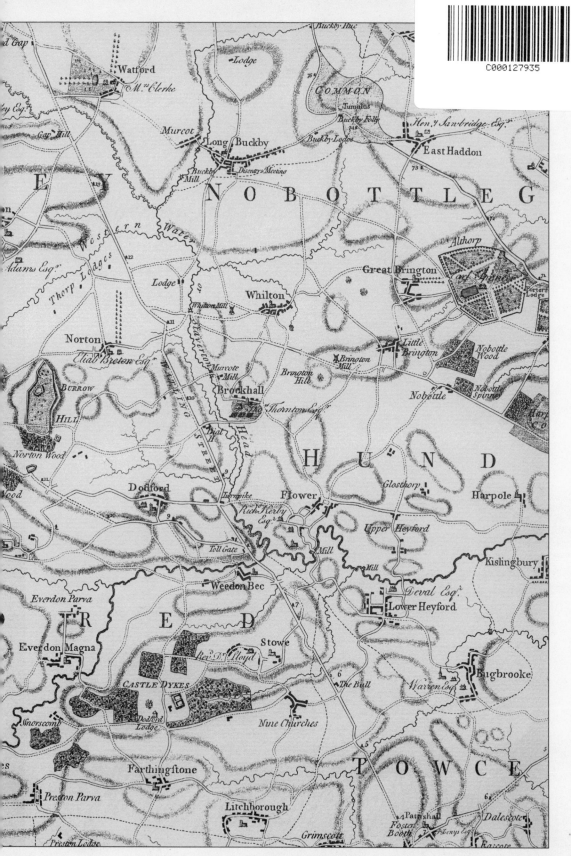

Daventry and district in 1791, from Eyre & Jeffrey's map.

DAVENTRY
PAST

Old Daventry, 1947, looking east along High Street

DAVENTRY PAST

R.L. Greenall

Phillimore

1999

Published by
PHILLIMORE & CO. LTD.
Shopwyke Manor Barn, Chichester, West Sussex

ISBN 1 86077 108 4

Printed and bound in Great Britain by
BIDDLES LTD.
Guildford, Surrey

Contents

List of Illustrations

Frontispiece: Old Daventry, 1947, looking east along High Street

Illustrations Acknowledgements

When some of the research for this book was being done 20 years ago I was given access to material in the Moot Hall looked after on behalf of the Charter Trustees by the late Mr. G. Moore and to photographs collected by him from the public. I made copies of them at the time to illustrate a future history of Daventry. Despite my best efforts, it has not been possible to locate the whereabouts of the originals, or the people who loaned photographs to Mr. Moore at that time. I therefore refer to them below, under 'Moot Hall collection/the late G. Moore'.

Illustrations are reproduced by kind permission of the following: Aerofilms, frontispiece and 91; A.E. Brown, 6, 7, 8, 13, 15, 41, 60; Colin Davenport, 18, 95, 96; Daventry and District Museum, 19, 31, 86, 92; Colin Eaton, 3; Moot Hall/the late Mr. G. Moore, 54, 67, 74, 76, 77, 78, 81, 83, 87, 88; Northamptonshire Libraries and Information Service, front endpaper, 1, 2, 17, 27, 32, 36 to 39, 42, 43, 45, 49, 55, 58, 61, 62, 65, 68, 71, 72, 80, 84. Nos. 12 and 48 were specially drawn by Northamptonshire Libraries staff in 1978; Northamptonshire Record Office, 21, 22, 40, 47, 49, 50, 51, 69, 82; Maps 89, 93 and the back endpaper are reproduced from Ordnance Survey 1:10,000 scale mapping with the permission of The Controller of Her Majesty's Stationery Office Crown Copyright; L.G. Tooby, 23, 24, 29, 44, 46, 59; United Reformed Church, Daventry, 56; Rev K. Ward, 26, 28, 33, 34. The following are from the author's collection, 4, 14, 25, 30, 35, 53, 66, 73, 75, 79, 85, 90; from Baker's *Northamptonshire*, 9, 10, 11, 20, 57; and from Bridges' *Northamptonshire*, 5, 16.

Acknowledgements

The origins of this book go back more than twenty years to a series of evening classes on the history of Daventry held in the winters of 1974 to 1978. The following people, not all of whom are, alas, still alive, put in at least two (and in some cases four) years' work on the records of the borough and the parish. Without their efforts this book would have been very difficult to write: Mr. D. Bond, Mrs. J. Dickens, Mr. B. A. Dymott, Mrs. J. Eaton, Mrs. A. Ede, Mrs. M. D. Faulkner, Miss K. Frost, Mrs. W. Larner, Mrs. P. Manchester, Mr. J. R. Meacock, Mrs. B. D. J. Moss, Mrs. C. Orr, Mr. G. D. Smith, Mr. A. Tooby, Mr. W. G. Tutcher, and Mrs. L. Wrentmore. The late Mr. L. B. Butcher and the late Mr. G. Moore were very helpful with material they had collected, particularly the latter who was a great gatherer-in of photographs. The major sources are in the County Record Office, where Miss Watson, and Mr. King before her, and their staff have been unfailingly helpful. The same is true of Northamptonshire Libraries, both at the Daventry branch, where Derrick Bond, a member of the group, was an indefatigable chaser-up of references, and at the Abington Street branch in Northampton, where Miss Arnold and Mr. Eaton have been very supportive over many years. I also record my thanks to Mrs. Angela Adams for information on St James' Church, to my colleague Tony Brown for permission to use maps from his *Early Daventry* (1991) and for discussions on Daventry, Mr. H. J. R. Wing of Christ Church, Oxford, for access to the records in his charge in 1977, to Mr. Colin Davenport for a copy of his MA dissertation on the Daventry Craft Companies, to the Rev. K. Ward, then rector of Daventry (whose wife was a member of the group) and to the Rev. K. L. Lee, then minister of the United Reformed Church, who both gave me access to their records. I should also like to express my thanks to Mr. L. G. Tooby for making the drawings of Daventry which illustrate this book, and to Mrs. Victoria Gabbitas of the Daventry and District Museum, Michael Goldsmid of the Daventry and District Society and David Walker for suggesting the book as a Millennium project, and to the Daventry District Council for generously grant-aiding its publication.

I should also like to thank Hugh Noyes, Esq. for permission to reprint the poem *Dane-Tree*, by Alfred Noyes, and the Ford of Britain Trust for help towards some of the illustrations used. Lastly, a special thank you to Kathryn Baddiley for all her labours with my endless corrections to the typescript of this book.

Supported by
Daventry and District Council's Millennium Fund

Foreword

I first visited Daventry in the late 1960s, soon after I came to Northamptonshire to work for the University of Leicester's Department of Adult Education. Daventry was then something of a 'Sleepy Hollow': walking down High Street that first day I would not have been surprised to find some local Rip Van Winckle asleep on the pavement. Yet, to the historian's eye, Daventry looked interesting: it exuded a sense of decayed importance. Its buildings, like those of any town, offered clues to its history—an old market place, an impressively wide main street, inns which had seen greater days, a Georgian town church and, as it turned out later, splendid historical records. Yet, on that day, looking at Daventry, something seemed to be missing. It soon became obvious what. Apart from the Burton memorial, the mock-medieval battlements of the BBC Club and a few old shop fronts, Daventry bore few signs of the transforming force of Victorian activity. It looked like what it was—an old, decayed road town to which the railway had failed to come in the 1830s, an event of such significance that it sent the place to sleep for over a century.

Daventry was about to be awoken. Moves between the Borough Council, Northamptonshire County Council and the City of Birmingham were already well advanced for a vast planned expansion, which, in the past 30 years, has come to fruition. For better and for worse 'Sleepy Hollow' has been transformed, modernised, New-Towned. Old Daventry is now encircled by hundreds of acres of new housing, industrial estates, roads, schools and colleges.

My original impression that Daventry might prove historically interesting was borne out in the 1970s, when I taught, or rather tutored, a series of evening classes on its local history. What we did was to work on the records of the borough from the Elizabethan charter to the coming of the railway. These records, housed mainly in the County Record Office, are magnificent in both quality and quantity, and their transcription and analysis kept a dedicated band of students busy for four winters. Our ambition was to produce a much needed history of Daventry. However, the course ran out of steam without having done any work on the early and medieval periods, or on the Victorian era and the 20th century. It so happened that my colleague, A.E. Brown, was working with adult education groups on the early history of the landscape in and around Daventry, and was eventually to publish his findings in *Early Daventry* (1991), the debt to which the early chapters of this book reveal. Over the years I pursued my own research into Daventry in the 19th and 20th centuries. We were both, of course, doing other things as well, but I never appreciated that it would be quite so long before the work could be brought together.

The stimulus to do so was provided by an approach from Michael Goldsmid and Victoria Gabbitas, on behalf of the Daventry and District Society and the Daventry and District Museum, to write an illustrated history of the town as a Millennium project. The Society and the Museum publicised the idea in Daventry and sought the grant from the District Council's Millennium Fund which has made the publication of this book possible.

This is a study of one of the small boroughs of England, the market centre of a rich agricultural district which, in the course of its history, found itself on one of the major roads of the kingdom. Until the last third of the 20th century, Daventry never was a populous place, though it was often a place of very good business. Patterns typical of English towns over the centuries are to be found here—origins as a rural settlement, emergence to urban status after the Norman Conquest, a period of growth and prosperity in the High Middle Ages, decline in the later 14th and 15th centuries, a slow and painful recovery in the Tudor century, Restoration and Georgian prosperity and Victorian decline. Despite this common framework, no two towns are alike. The historian's task is to tease out what is distinctive as well as what is typical and there are always variations in economic, social, religious and political patterns between one town and another. The identifying of these is what this book is about. The prime intention is, however, to provide for all those interested in Daventry, or in the Daventrys of this world, an up-to-date, readable and well-illustrated account of the long history of this Northamptonshire town.

One starting point might be to reflect on the role of planning, not just in the later 20th century, but over the long span of Daventry's existence. Historians find it useful to divide Lowland England into two distinct types of landscape: 'planned England' and 'unplanned England'. Northamptonshire, with its nucleated villages and its Anglo-Saxon open-fields which survived for eight or nine hundred years, is indisputably part of 'planned England'. Daventry's fields and Daventry's townscape did not evolve in the 'organic' way that the anciently-wooded landscape of districts such as Essex or the Weald of Kent and Sussex did, but as the results of a series of planning and re-planning decisions from ancient times to the present.

The Dane-Tree

By Alfred Noyes

Daventry calling … Dark and still
The dead men sleep, at the foot of the hill.

The dark tree, set on the height by the Dane
Stands like a sentry over the slain.

Bowing his head above their tomb
Till the trumpet rends the seals of doom.

Earth has forgotten their ancient wars,
But the lone tree rises against the stars,

Whispering, '*Here in my heart I keep
Mysteries, deep as the world is deep*'.

'*Deeper far than the world ye know
Is the world through which my voices go …*'

Daventry calling … Wind and rain
Against my voices fight in vain.

The world through which my messages fare
Is not of the earth, and not of the air.

When the black hurricane rides without,
My least melodies quell its shout.

My mirth and music, jest and song,
Shall through the very thunders throng.

You shall hear their lightest tone
Stealing through your walls of stone;

Till your loneliest valleys hear
The far cathedral's whispered prayer,

And thoughts that speed the world's desire
Strike to your heart beside your fire;

And the mind of half the world
Is in each little house unfurled.

Till Time and Space are a dwindling dream,
And my true kingdoms round you gleam;

And ye discern the thing ye crave—
That I do deeper than the grave;

I, the sentinel; I, the tree,
Who bind all worlds in unity,

So that, sitting around your hearth,
Ye are at one with all on earth.

Daventry calling: memory, love,
The graves beneath, and the stars above.

Even in my laughter you shall hear
The Power to whom the far is near,

All are in one circle bound,
And all that ever was lost is found.

*Daventry calling … Daventry calling …
Daventry Calling … Dark and still
The tree of memory stands like a sentry …
Over the graves on the silent hill.*

[This poem was written in honour of the official opening of the Daventry Station in 1925, and was broadcast during the inaugural ceremony.]

One

Daventry in its Local and Regional Setting

Daventry lies 12 miles west of Northampton, close to the border with Warwickshire. It is 20 miles from Warwick and the same distance from Coventry, 43 from Birmingham and 72 from London. Its immediate neighbours are (clockwise from the north-east) the parishes of Braunston, Welton, Norton with Thrupp, Newnham, Badby and Staverton. Over the centuries Daventry's economy came to rest on several bases. In origin it was a rural settlement, or, to be precise, two rural settlements, Daventry and Drayton, whose basis was agriculture, the parish having several kinds of soils, most of which produced excellent crops. In the later Middle Ages Drayton declined to the size and status of a hamlet, but retained its separate field system

until the middle of the 18th century, when it was enclosed by Act of Parliament, Daventry following suit half a century later.

The second and perhaps longest lasting of the bases of Daventry's economy was its function as a market town, serving the rich farming area which lay within a radius of about eight miles. Daventry's market began to flourish in the expanding economy of the 12th century, though it might well have had earlier origins. Despite local and national economic change over the centuries the town remains the shopping centre for its district to this day.

From medieval times Daventry's fortunes were also much affected by its location in the local and national road network of England. Through Daventry ran some important early routes, but it was in the Medieval era that lines of communication of major importance in Daventry's story came into usage, notably the roads from Northampton to Warwick and from Oxford and Banbury to Market Harborough and Stamford. Most significantly, from the 12th century, Daventry found itself on the great road from London to Chester when the line of that road route (now the A45) was diverted off Watling Street at Weedon to pass through Daventry on its way towards Coventry and thence to Birmingham and Chester. After 1800 this became the London to Holyhead road, the M1 of its day. Throughout its history the fortunes of Daventry were bound up with the state of inland trade. When this flourished, as it did in the era between the reigns of Queen Elizabeth and William IV, Daventry's innkeepers, horsedealers, merchants, shopkeepers and craftsmen did good business. When the basis of the transport system shifted away from the roads, as it did in the Victorian era, Daventry stagnated.

It did so despite the fact that, at the beginning of the 19th century, manufacturing, in the

1 Regional setting

form of footware, was established in the town. The making of boots and shoes for wholesale remained part of the local economy in a minor way until very recently, but never grew beyond a certain size. Daventry failed to become one of the major footware centres of Victorian Northamptonshire largely because the trade fell victim to the stagnation of the local economy following the failure of the main line of the railway to come to the town in the 1830s.

The parish of Daventry consists of 3,534 acres of once attractive undulating landscape. Its ancient boundaries are marked by well-defined natural features. Along the south by a series of prominent hills, on much of the west by a steep-sided valley, on the north and north-west by streams, and on the east by the elongated bulk of Borough Hill. Within the parish there is a

variety of soils. The hills on the eastern and southern rims, which rise to 653ft. in the case of Borough Hill and to over 700ft. in the case of Big Hill in the south-western corner, consist mainly of heavy Upper Lias clay capped on the top by Northampton Sand. A band of Marlstone outcrops along the lower slopes of the hills. This hilly part of the parish is bounded on the north-west by an area of lower ground consisting mainly of Middle Lias clays, and two streams, the North Brook and the South Brook, flow north-eastwards to a junction just north-eastwards of the site of Daventry town. To the north-west the land rises again over a Marlstone belt to a plateau reaching over 550ft. This plateau is covered with a sheet of heavy Boulder Clay with spreads of glacial sand and gravel around its edges. Daventry itself occupies the end of a

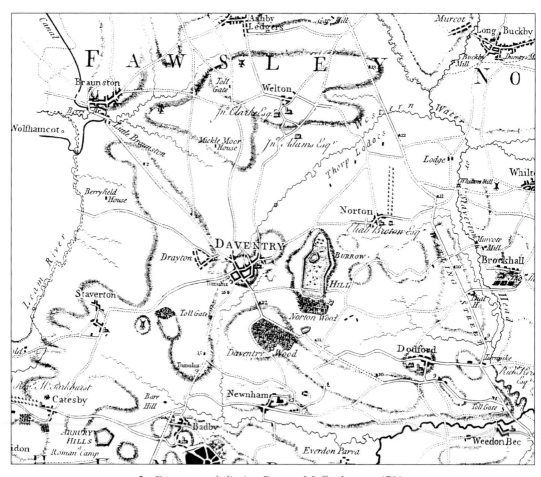

2   Daventry and district, Eyre and Jeffery's map, 1791.

3 Winter view of Badby village and Borough Hill (on horizon).

prominent (and defensible) spur projecting north-eastwards between the North and South Brooks. Its hamlet, Drayton, occupies a lower position a little way to the west in the valley of the North Brook.

Geographically, the parish of Daventry occupies a central position in a natural land unit centred on the headwaters of the River Nene, which rises on Arbury Hill in the parish of Badby immediately to the south. South-west of this, the terrain gives way to the valley of the Cherwell, and to the north-west to that of the River Leam. East of Daventry, on the other side of Borough Hill, lies the Watford gap. Although undramatic to the eye as a physical feature, this valley is the site of the remarkable bunching of lines of national communication—the Roman Watling Street (now the A5), the Grand Union Canal, the London and Birmingham Railway and the M1 motorway. Watford Gap is the natural route of communication from the

south-east of England into the West Midlands and to North Wales, first used by the Romans when they constructed Watling Street, their military road from London to Chester.

4 Daventry market in 1991. It has since been moved to High Street

Two

Under Borough Hill

The landscape of Daventry is dominated by Borough Hill, a long flat-topped eminence rising to over six hundred feet above sea level, in shape an elongated triangle some 134 acres in extent. Although much obliterated by modern farming and other activities, encircling the top of the hill was a set of ancient contour ditch and rampart defences and, within them at the northern end, another, smaller, clearly stronger set of defences. Current archaeological opinion is that the outer defences are possibly pre-Iron Age in origin, whilst the fort within the ramparts at the northern end is of the Iron Age.[1] Borough Hill is Northamptonshire's Maiden Castle, the largest of the county's ancient hillforts, greater in area than the real Maiden Castle in Dorset, though far less impressive archaeologically or visually. From the time of Camden onwards, Borough Hill has excited the imagination of antiquarians and archaeologists: it has always seemed to them to contain the secrets of man's ancient past in that district, and so it does.

Although the archaeology of Borough Hill has been investigated only piecemeal, enough has been found to demonstrate that it was a centre of local importance from earliest times. Palaeolithic implements have been found and, after the First World War, William Edgar, a local man, carried out field-walking and some excavation on Borough Hill and assembled 'a representative collection of flint implements' from within the hillfort—arrowheads, scrapers and worked flints of various kinds. In 1923 he published *Borough Hill (Daventry) and its History*, an account of his finds. Two Neolithic axes have been found, and palstaves from the Bronze Age. Over the years, Borough Hill has also yielded up a fair amount of Roman material. In 1823 George Baker, the Northamptonshire county historian, found pottery in a barrow south of the northern fort, and in his time a row of 18 Roman burial barrows

(which have since been destroyed) were investigated. The most impressive find from this period is a villa, or votive building, in the south-west corner of the northern fort, excavated by Baker, and re-excavated in 1852 by Beriah Botfield, squire of Welton. This yielded pottery sherds and other small Roman artefacts from the 2nd to the 4th centuries A.D., though only parts of this building were excavated. What seems likely is that the hillfort and villa or temple were the centre of a Roman land unit based on an older Iron-Age territory, of the kind that archaeologists and ancient monuments investigators have identified in other parts of the county. This in turn was probably the predecessor of the territory of the Roman town of Bannaventa, mentioned in the Itinerary of Antoninus. There was a time when it was thought that Daventry was Bannaventa (Weedon Bec being another suggestion). However, the site of Bannaventa has been located by modern archaeologists as lying across the line of Watling Street in the parishes of Norton and Whilton. No evidence of a Roman settlement has ever been found at Daventry itself, though scatters of Roman pottery have been found in archaeological field-walking on a good number of sites in the parish.

Although the origins of the present settlements of Daventry and Drayton are Anglo-Saxon, the hill undoubtedly had significance for the post-Roman inhabitants of the territory of Bannaventa. Four Anglo-Saxon graves have been excavated on Borough Hill, one from the Roman villa, yielding pottery and artefacts, and A.E. Brown speculates that Borough Hill could well have been the site of the pagan cult centre, *weoh dun* ('a hill with a temple or sacred place'), whose name later became that of the nearby village of Weedon.[2] Further possible indication of the hill as a post-Roman cult centre is the discovery of two Viking axe and spear heads buried there, not, apparently, associated with a burial. The myth of Danish origins is woven deep into Daventry folklore, partly because of the old ways of thinking that ascribed all ancient relics of the past to the Danes (so that the Iron-Age hillfort of Hunsbury Hill outside Northampton was known as 'Danes Camp') and partly because of the old dialect pronunciation of Daventry as *Daintry*, interpreted as *Dane Tree*. One result of this myth was that when Daventry became an Elizabethan borough the corporation seal was made in the form of a rebus, carrying an illustration of a curiously attired Dane, complete with helmet and battleaxe, grasping the branch of a tree. This Dane Tree device was to serve the corporation and borough council as their seal and 'coat of arms' until 1974. However, the tradition of an 'Old Dane Tree' is not entirely fanciful. Over the years the origin and meaning of Daventry's placename has proved something of a puzzle to scholars. The old folkloric Welsh *Dwy Avon Tre*, 'town of three rivers', favoured in Victorian times, has long been discredited. However, the *-tree* part of Daventry's placename is accepted, the modern interpretation

being that the origin of Daventry is *Dafa's Tree*, Dafa being the name of a founding father or paterfamilias. There almost certainly was an ancient meeting tree, probably on Borough Hill, though it seems more likely that it was an English rather than an old Dane tree.

Even after the focus of the settlement moved away, Borough Hill played more of a part in the life of the town than it has done since the beginning of the 19th century. It was used as common grazing when the fields of Daventry were still open, and on one day a year the cottagers of Daventry had the right to cut furze for fuelling on the hill. In 1645, shortly before the battle of Naseby, part of the army of Charles I camped there. In the 18th century Daventry race meetings were held on the summit, the course being within the circuit of the ditch and ramparts, and these meetings were much enjoyed in such a setting. However, public access to Borough Hill was effectively ended by the Act of Parliament in 1802 which enclosed the open fields. As in the rest of Daventry, the land on the hill was divided into closes bounded by quickset hedges, a

5 Engraving of Tillemans' drawing of Borough Hill in 1719.

farmhouse was built and the land brought under cultivation, perhaps for the first time. Baker and Botfield made their archaeological excavations shortly thereafter, but since their time much of the ditch and ramparts and the barrows they recorded and explored have been ploughed out. In this century the making of the golf course and the building of the BBC radio station continued the process of altering the surface use of Borough Hill and excluding the public.

One of the problems associated with archaeological finds in the past is that their significance is lessened because they were made by amateurs before, and sometimes long before, the development of modern archaeology. In particular, the recording of many of the finds is imprecise. This does not lessen the significance of the story they tell, but Borough Hill remains a major archaeological site which still awaits systematic examination, something which, in theory at any rate, is more feasible than hitherto, now that the BBC radio transmitting station has moved away. There have been recent trial excavations, but the many known sites, as well as sites so far unknown, await further investigation.

Three

Daventry's Origins and Early History

People who think about these things usually view the parish as the basic unit in the landscape, one which links us with the deep historical past. They are right to do so. When the Surveyor of Her Majesty's lands of the Duchy of Lancaster visited Daventry in 1571 to prepare a detailed survey of the manor, the first thing he did was to require a jury of 24 local men to describe the boundaries of the parish. They started at the north-east corner of the wood called the Parke, just south of the present London road near to the *Britannia* (formerly the *John o'Gaunt*) Hotel, and worked their way clockwise round the boundary, first going west, then north, then east, and finally south, along the lower slopes of the east side of Borough Hill, arriving back at 'the Parke Corner' where they had started. The bounds of the parish described in 1571 are the boundaries of Daventry today. Yet even in 1571 they were ancient.

Parishes, old though they are, evolved out of larger, even older land units. Reconstructing their history and evolution in the centuries before the Domesday Survey is a difficult business and calls for a combination of historical skills. The researcher has to be familiar with the lie of the land, best done by fieldwalking, ancient lines of communication and old boundaries, the discoveries of archaeology, the work of previous scholars in the field and the documentary evidence in Domesday Book and old charters. In the case of Daventry this work has been undertaken by A.E. Brown in his *Early Daventry* (1991), which, though complex and detailed, is a masterly piece of historical detective work.

One starting point is Domesday Book, what it says and how much of the evidence contained in it can be 'back-projected'. In 1086 Daventry lay in the hundred of *Egelweardesle*, one of two hundreds bounded on the east by the line of Roman Watling Street, the other being *Gravesende*.

These were later to be combined into the medieval double hundred of Fawsley, a unit of county government which was to have a very long life indeed, lasting until the 19th century. Brown argues that this double hundred was probably the successor of the estate once centred on the royal Mercian manor of Weedon, which, as *weoh dun* (hill of the sacred place), was, as already noted, probably successor to the former Iron-Age land unit based on the Roman villa on Borough Hill. Here at Weedon, St Werburga, the religious daughter of King Wulfhere of Mercia (658-75), spent much of her time. Later, perhaps after the Danish invasions, this estate came to be centred on the royal manor of Fawsley. The original centre of ecclesiastical authority in the district was the minster at Preston ('the priests' tun'), immediately south of Fawsley. When the focus of royal authority moved, it was followed by the ecclesiastical, the minster now also being located at Fawsley. Brown speculates that in these territorial arrangements there was possibly a third centre of importance, the place at which the king's reeve collected the rents and renders which were the economic basis of the royal estate.[1] This place may well have been Daventry. Centrally located in this postulated administrative unit, it had good communications with the surrounding vills, and some kind of official function, which would accord with what is known of the probable ownership of Daventry before the Conquest, seems possible.

By the time of Domesday Book these old, large administrative land units had been broken into smaller ones by the process of granting land to Anglo-Saxon thegns and churchmen. Nonetheless, there is evidence enough in Domesday Book and other medieval documents of older patterns of Anglo-Saxon settlement and ecclesiastical arrangements. Domesday Book records that the manors in Farthingstone, Everdon, Staverton, Braunston, Dodford, Welton and

6 The bounds of Daventry, as surveyed in 1571.

Thrupp all still lay within the soke or jurisdiction of Fawsley. A similar process had also gone on with regard to the authority of the minster at Fawsley, with the establishment of separate churches in some of the vills in its *parochia*, including, as we shall see, Daventry. There is, however, evidence enough in medieval documents that Fawsley was long regarded as the mother church of all the churches within the two hundreds of *Gravesende* and *Egelweardesle*.

The break-up of the large old units into the individual parishes we know so well was not necessarily at one step. Brown points out that Daventry once seems to have been part of a pre-Conquest religious unit and estate which consisted of Daventry, Drayton and Welton. The first mention of Daventry in any document is in Domesday

Book, but Drayton occurs earlier in a charter of 1021-3 describing the bounds of Newnham. Conversely, Drayton is not mentioned in Domesday Book, but is certainly there within in the entry for Daventry. Evidence that the township of Drayton had separate origins is clearly shown by the fact that the two places had their own field systems. That Drayton was always subordinate to Daventry is indicated by the fact that Drayton never attained independent parochial status, or even had a chapel of its own. In this respect it differed from Welton, which in the Middle Ages had its own church. However, for a long time Welton remained a chapelry of Daventry, and its parishioners had to bury their dead in Daventry until at least the late 13th century.

Apart from the burials on Borough Hill

7 Hundreds and parishes in the Daventry district.

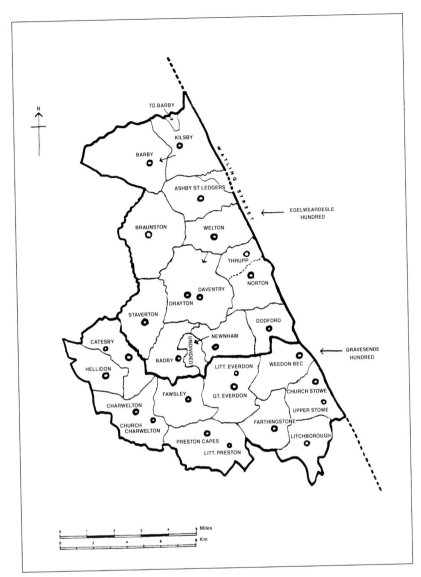

already noted, local archaeology has revealed few clues to Daventry's first Anglo-Saxon settlers. Little evidence of the pottery scatters which indicate the presence of Early and Middle Saxon farmsteads has been found in the fields, nor, in view of the extensive building in the present era, is there perhaps ever likely to be. But in the Late Saxon era the nucleated villages which remain to the present day the basis of the settlement pattern were created. Almost certainly the original vill of Daventry lies under the oval enclosure nowadays occupied by the church and churchyard. Why the scattered farmsteads of the Anglo-Saxons were

replaced by villages was probably due to growing numbers, the need for security and, most importantly, the need to organise a new system of arable farming. A recent archaeological excavation by a team from Northamptonshire Heritage produced the best indications so far of Daventry's settlement origins. This excavation took place in 1994-95, in St John's Square, near the new Leisure Centre. This site would have been on the downslope just below the ancient core of the town and had been used for the disposal of rubbish. On the evidence of what they found (most notably from some 875

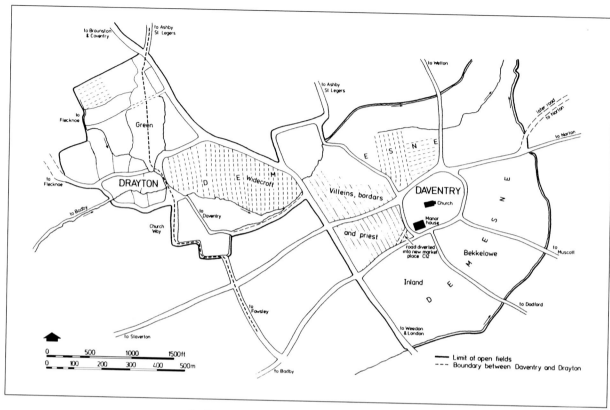

8 Daventry and Drayton before the Conquest.

fragments of pottery) they came to the conclusion that the site had been occupied in the 6th century A.D. and then, after a period of abandonment, was re-occupied in the 10th century. Occupation was then continuous, although it had waned from the 14th century, the site reverting to agricultural use.[2] This ties in very well with Brown's conclusions (reached from the use of quite different evidence) that Daventry's origins probably lie around the year 920, and also what is known about its medieval history. Interestingly, amongst the potsherds there was some evidence of even earlier occupation. Fragments from pre-5th-century vessels, a well preserved coin of A.D. 341-6 and some tesserae and Roman tile fragments were found, indicating the likely presence of a substantial Romano-British building nearby.

Not much is known about the origins of Drayton, which may well be as old, or nearly as old as Daventry, except that it was located on a low-lying site at the western edge of Daventry,

and probably had peasant origins. Using the evidence of medieval furlong names Brown is able to uncover some traces of the era before the creation of the open fields. For instance, the furlong name Dunstall, in the East Field of Drayton, derives from the old English *tunstall*, a farmstead. Brown suggests that the block of land from Tunslade southwards to the North Brook, to the north of the lord's demesne, was the original 'town' (ie. village) land shared and farmed by the villager of early Daventry. Grouped around the original core of Daventry were pieces of land the names of which belonged to ancient manorial tenants. One was a furlong called Reveland, which would have been farmed by the reeve who controlled their operations.[3]

Despite the myth of Daventry's Danish origins, and the unproven story that Borough Hill was the site of a last great battle between the Mercians and the Danes, nothing much is known about the district at the time of the Danish invasions. Not being situated on Watling Street or any other important route Daventry did not have the strategic importance of, say, Towcester, nor did it experience the sort of urban development Northampton underwent when it was made the base for a Danish army. The weapons found on Borough Hill seem to suggest that for the Danes it was the hill rather than any settlement below that had the greater significance, though these weapons are a merely a chance fragment of evidence. Nonetheless, the district certainly fell under Danish control in the second half of the 9th century. When the Treaty of Wedmore, which marked the successful end to King Alfred's war to contain the Danes, was made in 878, Watling Street was the line which marked the frontier between the Danelaw and that part of England which owed allegiance to the Kings of Wessex.

One of the most fascinating things that A.E. Brown is able to do is to map the lay-out of Daventry and Drayton. Clearly, the ancient core of Daventry was the result of the way that the tracks from neighbouring villages converged upon the defensible spur of land on which the town stands. By 1086 the street pattern was already there on the ground. High Street was the road from Staverton; the back lane (later New Street) was the road from Badby; and the line of the road from London, soon to become Newland (later Sheaf Street and Brook Street), was then the road from Weedon to Braunston. As yet there was no market place. In the south-west corner of the original manorial core stood the manor house. The tenements of the villagers and smallholders, who worked the lords's demesne, were laid out along both sides of the High Street, evidently the result of an earlier exercise in town planning.

When this took place is not certain, though in the course of his examination of the evidence Brown reaches two conclusions. The first is that the history of Daventry was conditioned by the fact that it lay on a block of demesne land and that the lay- out of its streets and fields was an act of deliberate manorial planning. The second is that this was probably done after the surrender of the Danish army of Northampton to Edward the Elder in A.D. 917. This was followed sometime after by the creation of the county of Northampton and the imposition of the first hideage (tax) assessment. The houses and tenements of the villagers and smallholders in place at the time of Domesday Book were laid out upon part of the lord's demesne. After the Conquest much of the demesne was given away, as we shall see, but one survival was the great close called the Inlands, the rump of a large tract which pre-dated, and never formed part of, the medieval open fields. Who the manorial lord was who oversaw these first planned developments of Daventry is not known: A.E. Brown suggests (projecting back from Domesday Book) that he was probably the Anglo-Saxon Earl of Northampton, lord of the great estate centred on Fawsley.[4]

Brown is able to demonstrate that part of this process was the laying out of identical field systems in Daventry and Drayton. Each contained 40 virgates (standard peasant holdings of 30 acres each), making two great fields of 1,200 acres each. In the Domesday Survey Daventry and Drayton were each assessed at 8 hides, which Domesday scholars have long assumed is a reduction of 60 per cent from the original, post 917, assessment of 20 hides, each hide originally containing 4 fiscal virgates.[5] What is remarkable is that, as well as instituting an agricultural regime which made possible the production of food for a growing population and was to last almost a millennium, the system was planned at the outset to fit the pattern of hidation (royal taxation). This was the arrangement which the Conqueror found *in situ*, took over, and by 1086 had modified. However, by 1086 the cultivated land of Daventry and Drayton had not reached its full extent. The next century and a half were to see a large-scale extension of land under the plough, which in turn involved a re-planning of the common fields.

Four

Priory, Manors and Market: Medieval Daventry

Domesday Book records that the Countess Judith, niece of the Conqueror, possessed the whole of Daventry, which was assessed at 8 hides (four each for Daventry and Drayton), that there were 12 acres of meadow, and that the whole had been valued in the reign of the Confessor at £3, but was now (in 1086) valued at £8. The Countess was the widow of Waltheof, an Englishman, who since 1065 had been Earl of Huntingdon and Northampton but who, in 1076, had been executed for rebellion against the Conqueror. The assumption is that Daventry had belonged to him as lineal successor as lord of that portion of the pre-Conquest royal estate based on Fawsley.

Brown makes the point that, at the time of Domesday Book, Daventry, with its total of 33 identified persons, was very similar in population and value to neighbouring vills. Norton (with Thrupp) had 34, Badby (and Newnham) 33, Staverton 24, Weedon 23, and so on. However, just over a century or so later, Daventry and Drayton had clearly grown in population and wealth more than their neighbours. The Subsidy Roll of 1301, for instance, contains 112 names from Daventry and Drayton, compared to 64 for Everdon, the next most numerous listing locally, and the trend of Daventry progressing faster than

its neighbours continued throughout the medieval period.[1] The reasons for this lay in some important developments in the early 12th century.

The Priory

The first of these was the founding of the Priory. For the background to this we need to return to the descent of the manorial lordship. In her widowhood it is said that William tried to bestow the Countess Judith in marriage to one of his French barons, Simon de Senlis, but she is said to have rejected him because of his lameness. What is certain is that, some time after 1089, de Senlis married her daughter, Matilda, and acquired the earldoms of Huntingdon and Northampton. Like many of his Norman contemporaries, Simon de Senlis was a great estate developer, a major figure in the history of Northampton, building the castle, expanding the town, and founding the Cluniac priory of St Andrew's, which became the principal religious house there. Almost certainly the example set by his overlord in Northampton influenced Hugh of Leicester, Countess Matilda's steward in Daventry, known as Hugh the sheriff, to found a small Cluniac

9 Daventry Priory seal, 1295. The figure is probably St Augustine.

priory beside his castle at Preston Capes. Soon after, about 1108, he moved his priory to Daventry.

There it was combined with the existing church in Daventry, a secular minster in the form of a college of four canons, priests endowed with their own prebends. It is not certain when the canons first came to Daventry, though it was probably post-Conquest. Nor is it known who was the founder. Before the canons, Daventry lay within the *parochia* of the minster of Fawsley. As already indicated, by the time of Domesday a smaller ecclesiastical unit of Daventry, Drayton and Welton had been formed out of the jurisdiction of Fawsley, part of the process of the break-up of larger into smaller units, the result no doubt of a growing population in the late Anglo-Saxon era. The researches of M.J. Franklin have revealed that Daventry college was endowed with the profits of the churches of Staverton, Welton, Cold Ashby and Braybrooke and a small amount of land in Daventry and several vills nearby.[2]

With the arrival of the Priory the arrangement was that the canons were given the choice of becoming monks or retaining their prebends during their lifetime. Two chose the former, two the latter. Hugh of Leicester, with the approval of Earl Simon and his wife, erected monastic buildings 'in honour of St Augustine, apostle of the English' next to the parish church, founding one of the major institutions in Daventry's medieval history. Not that the establishment of the Priory was trouble-free. The monks did not find it easy to

vindicate their title to the possessions of the canons, and in the early years the difficulties faced by the new house were exacerbated by the fact that, although the monks looked more to the Senlis Earls of Northampton as patrons than their founder, the earls remained lukewarm and were more committed to their own Cluniac house at Northampton. When the earldom passed into the hands of the Kings of Scotland the monks got even less support. The Priory was placed on a sound financial footing only when King Henry II granted it the ancient minster church of Fawsley.[3] After this, throughout the 13th century, Daventry's manorial lords and other pious people lavished gifts on it of property and church livings in Daventry and Drayton and some 24 other places, mostly in Northamptonshire. Although walled and gated from the town, as a major property owner, the Priory was a major influence on it.

On the religious front, the church served both parish and Priory, the parishioners having the use of the large south aisle, their part being physically separate from that of the monks. Some of the Priory's charters provide evidence of popular piety in medieval Daventry—the choice of the priory church as a burial place, alms given to the altar of St Mary, and devotion to the rood, which resulted in the re-dedication of the parochial part of the church to Holy Cross. As may be imagined, dual use of the church meant that relations between parishioners and monks were not always friction-free. If the church of Daventry was unusual in that only part of it was the parish's, the position of the parish priest was different from that in most other places. Under the canons the

10 Counterseal to **9**, probably the seal of Peter de Esseby, Prior in 1295.

cure of souls presumably had been per-
formed by them, though little is known
about arrangements then. Under the
Priory the position of the priest
was that he was one of two
chaplains appointed by the
house, one for Daventry
and one for Welton. His
status is unclear: Priory
charters refer to him as
chaplain, whilst the
Bishop of Lincoln's
registers on occasions
refer to him as vicar.
The truth is that the
priest of Daventry
was neither rector
nor vicar, and his
status was not
improved (though his
material conditions
perhaps were) when,
after 1435, the monks
appointed one of their
own number to minister to
the parish.[4] After the
dissolution this left the minister
of Daventry as a perpetual curate,
whose appointment was left to the
person who farmed the Daventry
estate of Christ Church in Oxford,
successors to the Priory
property. It was to take
a very long struggle
thereafter for the curates
to improve their stipend and status.

11   The seal of Nicholas de Ely, Prior of Daventry, 1231 to 1264.

consequence was that the road from London,
Watling Street, was diverted through
Daventry to Coventry and beyond. As
Brown points out, this altered the
local pattern of communications.
Earlier, the road which ran from
Northampton through
Staverton to Warwick, by-
passing Daventry, had
been the most important
route in the area.
Known as the port
wey, traffic from
London had joined it
at Weedon Bec.
When Coventry
became commercially
more important than
Warwick, the axis of
communication
moved north-west with
a new road (or the
upgrading of an old one)
through Daventry.[5] Thus
began Daventry's history as
a well-situated town, on the
road from London to the port
of West Chester. In the 12th
century Daventry developed into
the market town of its district. The
presence of a market is first attested
in 1203, though it
may well have
existed earlier. By
1330 Daventry also
had a fair, dedicated to St Augustine.

The Market

A second development, or set of developments, was the creation and planning of Daventry as a market town. Several factors lay behind this. The 12th and 13th centuries was a period of general economic expansion and growing population. By 1300 the cultivation of the land in England was pushed to limits not reached again until the time of the Napoleonic Wars. Agricultural surpluses led to the development of markets, markets led to concentrations of craftsmen in towns, and trade expanded nationally. All these factors played their part in the development of Daventry. In the early 12th century nearby Coventry rose to become a place of commercial importance. One

The Manors

One feature of considerable interest in Daventry's evolution as a town is the presence of burgages in High Street, first mentioned in a Priory charter of c.1148-66. It is not certain who first established them in Daventry, but they were undoubtedly part of a rearrangement of the layout of the town, one object of which was to create a market place, which was laid out immediately in front of the church. Another was to encourage people engaged in activities other than agriculture—craftsmen, shopkeepers, victuallers and other traders—to settle in the town, holding their property by the payment of rent, free from the obligation of agricultural service on the lord's demesne. Another

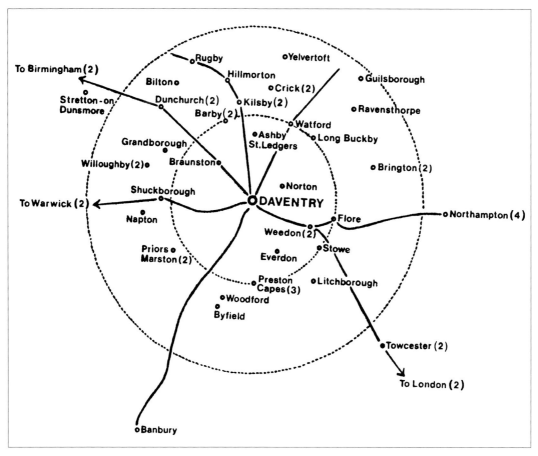

12   Daventry's market area. Carriers to places within radiuses of four and eight miles in 1831.

objective was to re-locate the villeins and bordars who worked the land. In order to understand these developments we need to return to the manorial history of Daventry. After Earl Simon's death, about the year 1111, Matilda married King David I of Scotland, who became Earl of Huntingdon and Northampton. About the year 1136, Simon de Senlis II, the son of the first Earl Simon and Matilda, succeeded to the earldom and Daventry became one of his possessions. On his death in 1153, passing down the female line as so often, Daventry went to his sister, another Matilda. That lady married twice. Her first husband was Robert fitz Richard, who died in 1136/7. Her second was Saher de Quincy, who became lord of Daventry by right of his wife in 1146. After Saher's death the manor passed to Walter fitz Robert, Matilda's son by her first husband,

and in 1198 in turn to his youngest son, Simon fitz Walter. Thereafter, the principal manor of Daventry remained in the fitz Walter family for nearly 200 years.

In the middle of the 12th century a substantial estate of 14 virgates, which became known as the Nether Manor, was separated from the main (Over) manor and granted to a local family, the de Daventres, who held it for nearly two centuries. However, in the late 14th century it ceased to have a separate existence. In addition to these two estates, as we have seen, the Priory constituted a third major property-holding corporation. Daventry was governed by the courts of these manorial lords. The Over Manor had a portmoot for its burgage tenants and the Priory a manor court; periodically agreements were entered into between the lay lords and the Prior about their

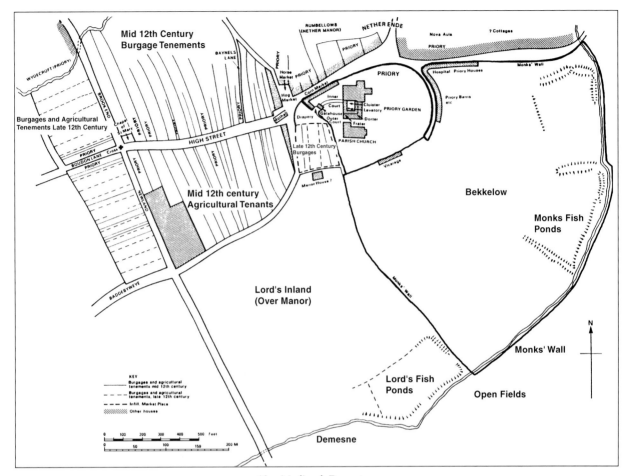

13   Medieval Daventry.

manorial rights over such matters as the monopoly of the bakehouse and the right to inflict fines and punishments for misdemeanours. The Nether Manor may also have had its court, but no record of it has survived.

A.E. Brown's researches show that it was around the middle of the 12th century, almost certainly in the time of Matilda de Senlis and her second husband, Saher de Quincy, that the replanning of the town took place, and this process may have been coincident with the creation of the Nether Manor.[6] Along the north side of the High Street, 14 burgage tenements were laid out, each with a 60ft. frontage. The fact that the boundaries of these typically long plots were, and in some cases still are, slightly curved and have this uniform width strongly suggests that they were laid out on lands once held and worked by

the villagers. On the other side of the street was a further set of 14 plots, again with 60ft. frontages, but these were not held in burgage: they were occupied by agricultural tenants.

At the close of the 12th century there was a further extension of the town along Newland (later Sheaf Street) and Brook End, along the street at right angles to the ends of High Street and Back Lane. Here, on the west side, a further 11 burgage plots were laid out in Newland and six in Brook End. Although they seem to have had the standard 60 ft. frontage they did not have the elongated backsides of those on High Street, being distinctively shorter in depth. In contrast to what the medieval documents refer to as 'acres in burgage' on High Street, these seem to have been nominally 'half acre' plots. Again, no document specifically records the creation of these

14 Junction of High Street, Sheaf Street and Warwick Street in 1974.

new burgages, but Brown's conclusion is that this additional development was the work of Walter fitz Robert, lord of Daventry, who died in 1198.[7] In other words, no great passage of time elapsed between the creation of the burgages in High Street and those in Newland and Brook End.

If these burgages were occupied by tenants of the Over Manor and the Priory, and the plots laid out on the south side of High Street by their villagers, where was the manor house and the houses and crofts of the tenants of the Nether Manor? Brown's researches indicate that they lay on the north side of the road to Norton now known as Abbey Street, between the roads to Ashby and Welton, in that part of Daventry referred to since at least the late 13th century as the Nether End. The manor house lay some-where north of these, its site being on a close known as the Rumbelows.[8]

With the growth in population continuing for about another century there was what might

be seen as suburban development beyond Nether End, along the road to Norton, which seems to have run as far as Sowbrook. As in most medieval towns it was the poor rather than the rich who lived on the fringes. These properties were cot-tages, mostly, but not entirely, owned by the Priory and occupied by people with perhaps a couple of acres in the open fields. Another example of 'suburban' development was a close north of the North Brook known as Widecroft, given to the Priory by Matilda de Senlis. When it was built-up with small tenements there was no break in the sequence of houses from the east end of Daventry to Drayton. In fact, by the beginning of the 14th century, as Brown points out, the built-up area of the town was greater than at any time until the early 19th century.[9] This, again, is not at all unusual in the long history of English towns. He also notes other develop-ments south and east of the church, near to the Priory fishponds. The presence of houses and a

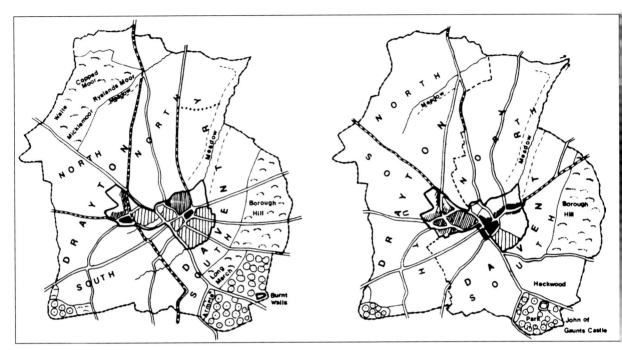

15   The Open Fields *c.*920 to 1290s (*left*), 1290s to *c.*1400 (*right*).

vicarage close to the churchyard are recorded within the area enclosed with a wall by the monks, known as the Bekkelowe. One of the consequences of the walling of their large precinct was the blocking off of the ancient trackway to Badby, which once ran across the Bekkelowe.

With the growth of the population of Daventry in the High Middle Ages there was a tendency for the burgages along High Street, Newland and Brook End to become subdivided or amalgamated. In the case of the property at the very end of the north side of High Street, where it joined Brook End, part was acquired for the chapel of St Mary, which did not survive the Reformation. Facing it, in the middle of the road at the junction of Newland, Brook End, High Street and Boudon Lane (later to become Tavern Lane, then Warwick Street) stood a cross, marking, perhaps, the end of the town's great market street. Other developments to be noted were, first, for the former agricultural plots on the east side of Newland to be built-up for shops and dwellings, with short property boundaries running, like the earlier ones on the other side of the street, from west to east. Secondly, as in many such towns, the market square was to be affected by in-fill,

reducing what was originally a large open space in front of the church to the small triangle which exists to this day.

Despite the fact that the manorial lords of certain villages close by, such as Long Buckby and Chipping Warden, secured market charters for these places, down to the 14th century Daventry flourished as a market town. Amongst its traditions was the belief that, in the reign of King John, it became a borough. The presence of burgesses and burgage tenure adds weight to the claim, such tenures being one of the generally recognised characteristics of boroughs. But was Daventry ever really a medieval borough? The most certain indication would be a charter from the King or manorial lord clearly granting privileges to the burgesses. No charter relating to Daventry earlier than that granted by Queen Elizabeth I in 1576 has ever been found, though the preamble to that document makes reference in a vague sort of way to ancient privileges granted by her progenitors. In the sense of having the sort of corporate powers of self-government it was later to acquire, Daventry was clearly not a borough such as Northampton was or even Higham Ferrers. It seems likely that Daventry's burgesses enjoyed the privileges of a seigneurial borough in an informal way, without these ever being formally confirmed. Certainly in the Subsidy lists of 1334 Daventry was taxed as a village not a borough.

With the growth of medieval Daventry demand for food led to the colonisation of the waste and an extension of land under the plough. Some indication of this process is illustrated by several of the furlongs in Drayton having *moore* names, indicating they were once rough, marginal land, and by such names as Long Marsh and Hackwood (ie. hacked wood) in Daventry Field. By the end of this process the only remaining pasture land in the parish was the expanse of Borough Hill. What Brown's researches show is that these new lands eventually prompted a complete re-planning of the open fields. Under this, the holdings of the virgaters were re-allocated in such a mathematically regular way, furlong by furlong, that it could only have been done anew at some specific point in time. The evidence indicates that this was in the late 12th century, at the time Walter fitz Robert was lord of Daventry. Almost certainly it was done when the new burgages were created in Newland and Brook End, and the Nether Manor given to the de Daventre family.[10]

The net result of the process was that each of the two field systems was increased by four virgates, so that there were now 44 virgates in Daventry and the same number in Drayton, and some further evidence of the deliberateness of the planning involved is shown by the fact that the boundary between the two townships was adjusted to facilitate this mathematical equality. For much of the High Middle Ages the arable land of Daventry and Drayton was worked under a simple two-field system, each having a North and a South Field, one lying fallow each year. However, from some time in the 15th century, the fields were re-arranged for the purpose of cultivation and a three-field system instituted.

Two features of the historic landscape of Daventry which have long been of interest to antiquarians are John o'Gaunt's Castle and Burnt Walls. The first, located in the south-eastern corner of Daventry parish, was what survived of the hunting lodge of the lord of the Over Manor's deer park. This park fell into disuse some time in the later Middle Ages. In the 1571 survey it was described as a coppice, and was grubbed up in the early 19th century. The hunting lodge had been a substantial building, with thick stone walls and a round tower surrounded by a moat, a fragment of which survives. This was what people later came to call John o'Gaunt's Castle. There is evidence that it had a predecessor close by, a low mound overploughed with ridge and furrow. And this too may have had a predecessor, the site on the other side of the London Road known as Burnt Walls. This is a triangular area defended by a bank and ditch on the west and on the north and south by the dammed water of a stream. Brown's researches show it was not there in the early 11th century. The ploughing-up of the Hackwood area in the period of the extension of cultivation in the 12th century probably led to its abandonment. The lodge was then moved to the site on the other side of the road, and ultimately rebuilt as an expensive example of the lordly passion for hunting the tall deer.[11]

Daventry in the later Middle Ages

By about the year 1300 the growth of the population, of land under the plough and of the economy generally reached their peak. Thereafter, there was a long period of setback, marked by plague and pestilence and a decline in the population. The great pestilence of 1348-9, the so-called 'Black Death', followed by a succession of other outbreaks, killed an estimated 30 to 40 per cent of the people. The 1377 Poll Tax listed 432 taxpayers (all people over 14, excluding 'paupers') for Daventry, and, extrapolating from this, it has been suggested that its peak medieval population (before 1348) was between 900 and 1000. Daventry's population, like that of most other places nationally, probably did not reach that again until two centuries later.

Little direct evidence for the local effects of the plague visitations survives. The deaths of beneficed priests in the Diocese of Lincoln in 1348-9 show that 30 per cent died in Daventry deanery as against 38 in Northampton, 43 in Rothwell and 54 in Higham Ferrers.[12] The fact that only 27 per cent died in Brackley deanery suggests that the Plague may not have been as severe in South Northamptonshire as in other parts of the county, though priests may not be a fair sample of mortality in the total population, and there were other visitations after this one. Manorial surveys and accounts of Daventry in the later medieval period and the first half of the

16th century reveal a shrinkage in the number of inhabited houses and the abandonment of cottages on the fringes of the town. Drayton was particularly affected. By 1381-4 it had become a shrunken settlement, with only six messuages left, 16 tofts being without the houses which had formerly existed upon them.[13] In time, Daventry was to recover and grow again, but Drayton remained shrunken. As late as the Henrician survey of 1530-32 there were many vacant plots and poorly maintained buildings in the town. Evidence from the open fields also reveals change resulting from the reduction of the population. In the 15th century the two-field system became a three-field system in both Daventry and Drayton, a move towards greater efficiency in that only a third instead of half the land lay fallow each year. Another development was that parts of the fields ceased to be used for the cultivation of arable crops and were put down to grass, particularly on the periphery. One of the greatest changes that the 15th century brought was the abolition of the feudal services demanded of the peasants, and the converting of customary tenures to freehold or copyhold or the payment of money rents, though when this happened in Daventry is not known with certainty. The shrinkage of the late medieval economy also had its effects on local trade and retailing. Market villages like Long Buckby, Chipping Warden and dozens of others in Northamptonshire ceased to attract buyers and sellers, and their markets decayed away. Daventry's, however, did not, though business carried on at much lower levels than before.

There is some evidence that the Priory did not escape the effects of the economic decline of the era. In 1442 Prior Robert Man was arraigned before the Bishop of Lincoln. Amongst the many accusations made against him by his convent was that he had allowed many of the Priory properties to fall into decay, in spite of previous warnings. This was seen as the result of his personal shortcomings but was probably also due to the economic decline of his time. There being more profit in wool than corn, one way of adjusting to changing conditions was to go in for enclosure. In 1489 the Prior enclosed Thrupp in Norton, where he destroyed 18 houses, abandoned the chapel and converted 400 acres of arable to pasture. By 1564 there was only one house left on what was now Thrupp Grounds. In 1495 the prioress of the religious house there did something very similar in Nether Catesby. Daventry Priory had seen difficult times in another direction since the early 13th century, when it had been gradually separated from its mother house, La Charité sur Loire, and assimilated into the Benedictine Order, in which it perhaps never enjoyed more than minor prestige. Although it may not have realised it, by the early 16th century it was in an increasingly vulnerable position.[14]

The later Middle Ages also saw changes in Daventry's manorial history. When the male line of the family failed in the later 14th century, the Over Manor was divided between two surviving fitz Walter sisters. One portion was ultimately transferred to John of Gaunt, Duke of Lancaster, and the other was sold in 1398 to his son Henry, Duke of Hereford and Earl of Derby, later King Henry IV. The Nether Manor retained its separate identity during the 13th and 14th centuries, but some time before 1372-3 was also acquired by John of Gaunt, and, like the main manor, passed to his son, Henry. In this way both Daventry manors were brought together again and became part of the Duchy of Lancaster. In the 15th and 16th centuries the steward of the Duchy was a powerful figure in Daventry.

Five

'Baily Town': Tudor and Stuart Daventry

The Dissolution of the Priory

In Daventry, as elsewhere, the prolonged decline of the medieval economy lasted until the second half of the 16th century. Indeed there is some evidence that it was worse in Daventry than in other Northamptonshire market towns. Under Henry VIII's Lay Subsidy of 1524, only 92 tax-payers were recorded for Daventry, less than in any town except Brackley.[1] The picture of de-cline in Daventry is underlined by the Duchy of Lancaster survey in 1530-32, which mentions many vacant plots and poorly maintained build-ings.

The dissolution of the Priory, one of the major events in the town's history, can only have made the economic situation worse. The end of its 400-year history pre-dated Henry VIII's gen-eral suppression of England's religious houses. Daventry's monks fell victim to Cardinal Wolsey's grand scheme of founding a new college in Oxford in the 1520s. Wolsey's agents made demands upon the Priory for certain lands to endow this foun-dation. The monks refused but England's most powerful politician had no trouble in obtaining papal sanction for the closure of the Priory and the diverting of its endowments. The Priory was granted to him in 1526, and closure went ahead, though Wolsey's scheme did not. The Cardinal's failure to secure for Henry VIII an annulment of his marriage to Queen Katherine led to Wolsey's disgrace and fall in 1530. The progress of the new college was arrested and revenues appropri-ated to it were seized by the Crown. In 1532 a plan for the college was re-started by Henry VIII, and the Priory of Daventry with all its posses-sions was included in the endowment, and con-tinued annexed to it until the next development, when the dean and canons of Christ Church surrendered to the king in 1545, preparatory to the college being converted into a bishopric. In 1546 the college was revived for a third time

with the title of 'the Cathedral Church of Christ in Oxford'. In this development, much of the property and endowments of the Priory outside Daventry were diverted to other uses. However, its assets in Daventry, consisting of the great and small tithes, 16 yardlands, a number of closes and pasture grounds and certain houses and gardens, including the Abbey House, became part of the estates of Christ Church.[2]

From the start it was the practice of the dean and chapter to farm out the whole of the estate in Daventry, together with Thrupp Pastures, to a single tenant, who then sublet. As possessor of the tithes, the tenant of Christ Church was re-sponsible for finding a curate for Holy Cross, a far from satisfactory arrangement. The first tenant was Thomas Andrew of Charwelton and for half a century the estate was leased to him and his heirs and successors. Some time before 1598 the tenant became one Powel Isacke. Then, from 1649 to 1751, successive members of Daventry's leading family, the Farmers, were in possession.

The estate records of Christ Church reveal that in the first year of the reign of Edward VI Robert Andrew was college tenant and also bail-iff of the manorial court of the Priory, granted to the college at the foundation. A memorandum of c.1598 notes that Andrew, who had the bailiwick for 99 years, had held the courts in the time of Queen Mary and that there were many copyholds. The college has records of the court being held until 1608, after which date no evidence of its existence survives. Perhaps the land became lease-hold and was merged with the other college property.[3]

The Reformation in Daventry

The dissolution of Daventry Priory had nothing to do with the Henrician assault on the Catholic Church, though it was a portent. There seems little evidence of early protestantism in Daventry.

16   Engraving of Tillemans' drawing of Daventry church and the Priory remains, 1719.

On the contrary, religious bequests made in early 16th-century wills give a sense that traditional piety continued unchanged in the last years of medieval Catholicism. They contain donations to the altars, images and lights in St Augustine's and Holy Cross. There were requests to be buried within the church before the Rood, and George Robinson in 1527 left six shillings and eight pence for a processional banner with the picture of St George on it, 'to be borne on the crosse daies'. The altar and chapel of the religious guild of the Trinity and Holy Cross were remembered, as was the chapel of St Mary which stood at the western end of High Street. There were also bequests to the bells of Daventry, and for the saying of special masses.[4]

In the 1530s and '40s came 'the stripping of the altars'. All the accoutrements of catholic ritual were swept away. Roods were removed from rood screens, images removed, wall-paintings whitewashed over and much painted glass destroyed. The doctrine of purgatory was abandoned, and the assets of chantries seized. In the absence of churchwardens' accounts and other

such records all too little is known about what happened in Daventry given the changes of direction taken by religion in the reigns of Henry VIII, Edward VI or Queen Mary. Because of the unsatisfactory arrangement whereby the appointment of a curate was left to the tenant of Christ Church and needed no formal institution by the bishop, the names of the clergy can only be recovered from wills which they witnessed and this is all that is known of them. Between 1526 and 1559 the names of seven men appear. Then there was Ralph Phillips from 1559-61.[5] It may well be that Phillips was the first protestant curate, being appointed in the same year as Queen Elizabeth's Act of Uniformity, which defined the form and doctrine of the Church of England.

How did the apparently devoutly catholic Daventry of the time of Henry VIII become the apparently zealous protestant Daventry of the reign of James I? One reason was that religious change was ruthlessly imposed from above. Another was that in the reign of Queen Elizabeth Daventry became a puritan centre (puritans being 'the hotter sort of protestants'). In part this was the result of the encouragement and protection given to them by certain of the local gentry, above all Sir Richard Knightley. Its geographical position made it a natural home for puritan ideas, there being an observable connection between wayfaring, fairs and markets and the dissemination of new religious ideas. The 20 years from 1570 saw their spread within Northamptonshire. The thrust of puritanism was the spreading of protestant doctrine amongst an often poorly educated and ill-paid clergy. There was also dissatisfaction with the Elizabethan religious settlement, both in respect of theology, forms of service and the government of the church. For the hotter sort of protestants, religious reform had not gone far enough in 1559. Such matters as bowing, kneeling and the wearing of the surplice were avoided, and some began to voice criticisms of bishops and diocesan structures. Activity began with the exercises and services known as 'prophesyings' and among the diocesan records there is the presentation of 16 lay people from Daventry accused of travelling to Southam in Warwickshire, a noted early centre of these prophesyings. In the 1580s the puritan ministers in the county divided themselves into three classes, at Northampton, Kettering and Daventry. Here they tried out a proto-presbyterian organisation within the church of England. The *classis* at Daventry has been described as 'a cohesive group of Knightley proteges', consisting of the incumbents of Byfield, Fawsley, Charwelton, Plumpton, Culworth, Preston Capes and Weedon Bec. However, the minister of Holy Cross was not among them. With the accession of Archbishop Whitgift to the primacy in 1583 much tighter control was exercised over parish clergy by the church authorities. Although the archbishop was strongly supported by the Queen, he had enemies in Parliament and the puritan gentry. One reaction came in the form of the Marprelate tracts attacking episcopal persecution of the godly. Printed on a press which was peripatetic to evade detection, it was at Fawsley in November 1588, then at a farm house in Norton by Daventry, whence it moved north. The authorities caught up with it near Manchester. At this stage puritanism seems stronger outside Daventry than in, especially at Fawsley where the Rev. John Dod, famous for his *A Plain Exposition of the Ten Commandments*, dwelt long under the pa-

Ob. An Ch.1645.

Ætatis suæ 96.

A Grave Divine; precise, not turbulent;
And never guilty of the Churches rent:
Meek even to sinners; most devout to GOD:
This is but part of the due praise of DOD. C.B.

17 John Dod, the puritan divine. Vicar of Fawsley, 1624-45, he lived to be 96.

tronage of the Knightleys.[6] If so, it was not to stay that way very long. The laity of the town were to fall under the discipline of the godly, laid down upon them by the town authorities.

One new Daventry institution was intended to play its part in the spread of protestant ideas. In 1576 a Grammar school was founded by William Parker of London, woollen draper, a native of Daventry, who settled upon a master £20 a year for ever to instruct 50 scholars in Latin free of charge. A further provision in his will gave £10 a year to be distributed among six poor men. After resisting the efforts of the widow and her new husband to divert the endowment to their own uses, money was raised in Daventry to erect a schoolhouse, which was opened in 1600. Wase tells us that in the late 17th century Parker's benefaction was remembered by an inscription on the wall of the church and a painting of six beadsmen in their gowns, lost when the church was demolished in the next

18 The Free Grammar School, New Street, built
1600, restored 1857.

century. The schoolhouse they built in New Street
was not and survives to this day, though it long
since ceased to house the school.[7]

Both catholics and puritans hoped for much
when King James VI of Scotland became James
I of England in 1603. They were both to be
disappointed. There were to be no changes to
the Book of Common Prayer or the structure of
the church, and there was to be no toleration for
catholics. In their disappointment and outrage
some young hotheads from leading recusant
families in this part of the Midlands—
Throckmortons, Catesbys and Treshams—hatched
the Gunpowder Plot. They were ruthlessly hunted
down. In November 1605 Matthew Young,
keeper of the *Bell* Inn in Daventry, testified before the magistrates that some of them had met
on his premises a month before the plot was
discovered.[8] The Elizabethan laws against popery
and recusancy were renewed. Puritans fared better.

Despite the attitude of the government, their cause
widened its support within the laity, not least in
strongly governed towns such as Daventry.

The incorporation of Daventry

From about the second decade of the reign of
Queen Elizabeth I the economic situation in the
country was showing marked signs of
improvement. The population was growing, trade
improved and the fortunes of market towns,
especially those on the main roads of the kingdom,
began to prosper again. In Daventry, the survey
of the town in 1571 made for the Duchy of Lancaster, known as the Dragge Book, shows clearly
that houses in decay or untenanted in 1530-32
had in many cases now been rebuilt or re-occupied. This is borne out by the surveys of 1591 and
1617-18 which refer to many newly erected houses
and cottages. As one historian of this period points
out 'market tolls suddenly became an important
source of revenue; half-forgotten customs of urban freemen began to take on a new significance'
and towns began to seek powers to modernise
their government.[9] This was certainly the case in
Daventry. In 1571 a petition signed by John
Farmer, John Spencer, Richard Knightley, Edward
Onely and Thomas Spencer was addressed to the
Earl of Leicester referring to a suit made by John
Symes and others for the incorporating of the
town. The signatories represented the opposition
to John Symes on behalf of his nephew, Richard
Symes, 'now farmer and bailiff (of the Duchy of
Lancaster) there'. They argued that if John Symes'
suit for incorporation was successful 'the good
estate of the towne and market which at this
present is suche as in all these partes there is no
better' would be harmed. They declared that John
Symes and others had joined themselves together
to press for incorporation 'for there private com-
modity, being great freeholders within the same
towne: and some of them Intruders upon the
quenes Majesties Inheritance'. Clearly there was a
power struggle going on within Daventry and the
Symes (or Symmes) family were at the centre of
it. The 1571 Dragge Book shows that both were
considerable owners and occupiers of property,
and a William Symmes appears in Henry VIII's
Lay Subsidy of 1524 as one of the larger taxpayers. It is possible that this was the man whose
mutilated brass John Bridges noted in the parish
church in the early 18th century. This depicted a
man and his wife and their five sons and five

19   Portrait of Elizabeth I in the first letter of her charter of incorporation, 1576.

daughters. The fragment which remained said that this William Symmes died in 1547. Possibly he was the father, or grandfather, of the 'great freeholder' who aspired to be Daventry's chief magistrate in 1571, and who achieved that position five years later.[10]

Writing in the early 18th century, Bridges calls Daventry a 'Baily town'. By then, its chief magistrate was a bailiff, who presided over a corporation of 14 burgesses and 'twenty men of the commonalty' established under Queen Elizabeth's charter of 1576. However, the Account book of the Bailiffs of Daventry (which commences in 1574) indicates that in the period immediately before the charter the town was governed by two bailiffs. There is no mention of burgesses or members of the commonalty. The account book also makes clear that in these two pre-charter years the craftsmen of Daventry were organised into companies, the Elizabethan form of guilds.[11] The question arises whether these arrangements had an existence back into the medieval past, or were of recent origin.

20   The seal of the borough, 1595.

The preamble of the Bailiffs' account book indicates that it was the latter, because it praises Lawrence Eaton (or Eyton) of Brockhall for securing the two-bailiff arrangement. This may well have been a compromise between supporters of the traditional manorial supremacy of the Duchy of Lancaster and the aspirations of other leading burgesses for stronger powers of self-government. The craft companies were no doubt formed in accordance with the recent Statutes of Apprentices and Artificers. The fact of their formation argues for the imminence of borough status, because only boroughs possessed powers to regulate guilds. The Bailiffs' account book also contains a memorandum, dated 1 May 1575, reflecting the interest of the Crown in Daventry because of its growing position on the great road to Chester. It lists the names of 49 leading inhabitants, headed by Mr. Andrews, 'Bayley Roper' and 'Bayley Salter', each agreeing to find a post-horse for royal business 'when his turn cometh or pay six pence to him that shall go for him' upon pain of 20 shillings for every default.

This account book records that on 29 September 1576 only one Bailiff, John Symmes, was chosen and that he took his oath before a newly appointed Recorder. The same page also lists the names of the first burgesses and members of the commonalty. The period of the town being presided over by two bailiffs was over: a borough charter obtained from Queen Elizabeth now became operative.[12] Whether or not it represented a triumph by John Symmes over the friends of Lawrence Eyton is unclear. Whatever its origins, the system it introduced was to last upwards of two and a half centuries. The charter's preamble recalls dimly-remembered history, Daventry's long decline and recent efforts to secure a form of local government agreeable to the leading parties in the town. Daventry was to be headed by a body corporate, able to sue and be sued. It was to seal any legal agreement with a common seal, which could be broken and remade. The design on the seal, an Elizabethan-looking Dane grasping the branch of a tree, married myth, modernity and history and was used as long as Daventry had borough status. The corporation had the power to regulate and make bye-laws for the 'rule of Artificers and other inhabitants and residents' which, until the reign of Charles II, it devolved to several craft companies. The first members of the corporation and the first Recorder were all named in the charter. John Savage was Bailiff, to hold office until Michaelmas that year (when John Symmes succeeded). The Recorder was John Daffarne, who had the office for life. The Bailiff and Recorder were to be Justices of the Peace for the borough, and the year after his bailiwick the ex-Bailiff was to be coroner. The Bailiff and 14 burgesses were to constitute the common council, Mr. Bailiff was to be clerk of the market, and the borough was to have two Sergeants at Mace, appointed for life.

A sure sign of Daventry's rising level of business was the fact that, in addition to the ancient weekly market and fair on St Augustine's day (26 May), two new three-day fairs were granted— Easter Tuesday (and the two days following) and St Matthew's day (21 September and the two days following), together with courts of piepowder for the immediate settlement of disputes arising. These new fairs belonged to the corporation and not to the lord of the manor. For the right to hold them the corporation had to pay 6s. 8d. yearly to the Crown. A fortnightly court of Record was to be held before the Bailiff and Recorder (or his deputy) and the Moot Hall was to be the place where the corporation and courts met. The charter detailed the way Bailiffs and Recorders were to be elected, how they were to be replaced if they died in office, and how men nominated to the corporation were to be punished if they declined to serve. The essential character of the corporation was that it was 'closed'; elections to it were in the hands of the corporate body itself and not in those of any wider electorate. It was also powerful, having the right to punish anyone disobedient to its dictates. The charter also granted privileges to Daventry vis-à-vis the world beyond. No 'foreigner' could serve on any jury within the borough, and no inhabitant could be impanelled on coroners' juries outside Daventry or a jury of the Assize. This concept of being a little world within the wider realm was underlined by the economic philosophy that, within corporate boroughs, the workings of business and trade were best regulated by craft companies licensed by the corporation. This medieval concept, revived by the Tudors, believed it was better to divide and regulate the market rather than having competition within it. One thing which did not follow incorporation in Daventry was that it never became a parliamentary borough. Why it should have failed where Brackley and Higham Ferrers succeeded is not apparent. It may have been a matter of timing, these places being given borough status earlier, or it may have been that Daventry did not have any great magnate behind it with an interest in promoting its representation in Parliament.

As we have seen, the organisation of craft companies pre-dated the borough corporation. The Bailiffs' account book records their early history down to 1590, when the companies were reorganised and began to keep their own records

separately. In the early years the grouping of Daventry's craftsmen and traders presents a shifting scene. At first there were six companies, then five, when the mercers joined the woollendrapers, tailors, weavers and fullers. It is easy to see why shoemakers and tanners were grouped together, and butchers and victuallers, but why the smiths and husbandmen (farmers) were united in a fourth company, and leathermen and glovers with carpenters and masons in a fifth, is less apparent. The lack of compatibility between certain of the crafts, and the smallness of some these groupings, probably lay behind Bailiff Richard Farmer's survey of them in 1589 and the replanning which followed the next year. Farmer listed the different trades in three groupings—68 shoemakers, tanners, whittawers and smiths, 52 mercers, woollendrapers, linendrapers, fullers and innkeepers, and 103 husbandmen, victuallers, dyers and weavers. The restructuring of 1590 grouped them somewhat more rationally. The leather and metal trades were brought together as the company of shoemakers, ironmongers, saddlers, barber surgeons, smiths, glovers and whittawers. A second company was made up of people engaged in making or dealing in textiles—mercers, drapers, haberdashers, tailors, dyers and weavers. And a third was formed out of the building trades. Two callings, formerly included in craft companies, were excluded—husbandmen and victuallers.

Although Daventry's history as a borough began in 1576, for almost four centuries its seal bore the date 1595. It is clear that the creation of the corporation was a development with such important consequences that these took time to be accepted and enforced. The re-organising of the craft companies by Bailiff Farmer was part of this process. In the borough records are Letters Patent of 1590 which summarise a case brought by the Attorney-General against the inhabitants of Daventry accusing them of using certain franchises and liberties without warrant or royal grant.[13] In their defence the charter of 1576 was produced. This was accepted and Letters Patent of 6 May 32 Elizabeth (1590) were granted. It is not altogether certain that these proceedings were genuine. It is just possible that the corporation were making doubly sure by seeking to have the main text of the charter enrolled in court records as well as the Patent rolls by a fictitious suit. On the other hand, in the court proceedings they were addressed as 'the inhabitants of Daventry',

21 Two ordinances from the Book of the Company of Mercers, 1590-1676 (NRO 696). No.6 reads: Item yt ys ordayned established and decreed by the mutuall Assent & consente of the artyficers of taylors dyars ffullers and weavers that whosoever hee bee that ys freed bee he eyther townesman or stranger before hee dothe sett upp to worke of any of the occupations aforsayde, shall paye for his freedome fyve pounds. No.7 reads: Item yt ys ordayned established & decreed that whosoever hee bee that ys made free of anye of the occupations Aforesayde shall paye to the chamber of the towne Tenne shillings except such as have served their whole apprentyshippe in this towne.

implying that they were not recognised as a body corporate. In 1595 the corporation sought a ruling before two of Her Majesty's Justices of Assize under a statute made in the 19th year of the reign of Henry VII against the 'multitude of foryners and dwellers out of the same borough' coming into Daventry and plying their trades at other times than market or fair days, 'never beinge apprenticed, privileged or freed within the same'. What aggrieved the freemen of Daventry was that these outsiders were avoiding payment towards charges borough freemen were liable for, in particular 'maintaining the queen's service with post horses towards Ireland', the cost of erecting a school house for a free Grammar School and the relief of the poor.[14] They duly got what they sought; an ordinance limiting the practice of any art, mystery or trade within the borough to those

who dwelt there and had been apprenticed, or had purchased their freedom, and the power to fine for transgressing this ruling. The exceptions were:

> that it shall and may be lawful for all needful butchers, fishmongers and other victuallers for the sale only of their flesh, fish and victuals to come and repair to the said market town and borough on all fair and market days at their pleasure.

Outside traders and craftsmen, 'strangers' or 'foreners' who wanted access to Daventry's market and fairs could only have it by purchasing their freedom, and there were always a good number in this category. The only exceptions were all 'burgesses, merchant men, citizens and inhabitants of the city of Coventry' who, under letters patent

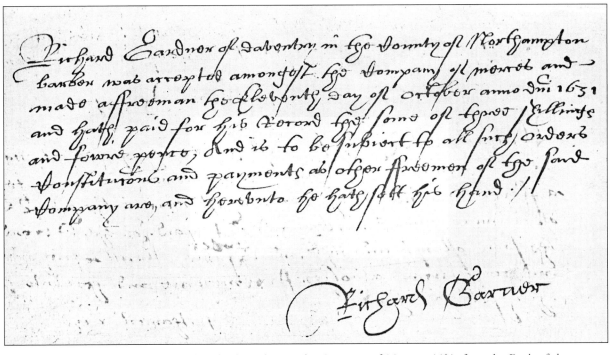

22 Record of the freedom of Richard Gardner in the Company of Mercers, 1631, from the Book of the Company of Mercers 1590-1676. It reads:
Richard Gardner of Daventry in the County of Northampton barber was accepted amongst the Company of Mercers and made a ffreeman the Eleventh day of October anno domini 1631 and hath paid for his Record the some of three shillings and fowre pence. And is to be subject to all such Constitutions and payments as other ffreemen of the said Company are and hereunto he hath sett his hand. [signed] Richard Garner.

granted by Queen Elizabeth in 1603, were allowed to trade in Daventry toll free and without the obligation to serve their apprenticeship in Daventry or take up their freedom. The ordinance gave the corporation power to levy on every inhabitant and freeman scot and lot, taxes for the above purposes. These developments gave the borough a new start. With the clarification of its status and powers the old seal was broken and a new one made. Since 1591 the Recorder who had been intimately involved in these processes had been Thomas Thornton of Newnham. Such was his success in the law that in 1625 he was able to purchase the manor and advowson of Brockhall. The first Thornton of Brockhall remained Recorder until his death in 1632, establishing what became a long family connection with the borough.

Beginning in 1595 the Borough Assembly Book records a series of decisions to enforce the above regulations regarding who should be free to follow their trade in Daventry, and the terms

on which traders using the markets were to operate.[15] One in 1597 required all brewers of ale to sell it at 2d. a quart until further notice. Another appointed one man from each of the craft companies to go round the market on market days to 'give intelligence unto the bailiff for the time being of all such tradesmen as use any mystery or trade, and not being freemen of the said borough, to the intent that order may be taken with them, either that they may be freed or expelled the market'. Another concerned the Sexton's duties, which included the ringing of a bell at 5 of the clock in the morning, a 'fourth bell' at 9.00pm, ringing on Sundays, Holy days and lecture days, keeping the town clocks in good order and keeping the church and seats in a better and more orderly manner than hitherto, upon pain of dismissal.

Local Government in the 17th century

The next development in Daventry corporation's history was the surrendering of the charter to

King James in 1606 and his re-grant. One consequence was that a far more elaborate and detailed set of orders and constitutions, 51 in number, were drawn up. They reflect a well-developed sense of civic pride and set out for their successors in the Moot Hall borough customs established over the past three decades. What is noticeable is the incorporation of the vocabulary and values of puritanism. Despite the efforts of the government and episcopate, this particular religious outlook was spreading generally within the church, notably in corporate towns. The first eight constitutions are all about religious observance. Every person on the corporation was to go in his gown to the parish church at Christmas, Easter and Pentecost and every Sabbath day, morning and evening. Churchwardens and constables were to see that everyone in the borough who could attend, did attend church every Sunday, and that there was no profaning of the Lord's day by the playing of unlawful games, pastimes and sports. There was to be no working, shops were to be shut, millers were forbidden to fetch and carry corn from suppliers, and there was to be no commencement of journeys to distant places or fairs on the Sabbath. Each order carried a fine for transgression. Daventry, as a market town, was not a place where cakes and ale were noticeable by their absence and there were tensions between the godly elite and the frequenters of common alehouses. In the 17th century fines for drunkenness and swearing became a reliable if minor source of income for the corporation. The promotion of godliness was furthered by the institution of the lecture, a weekly sermon or exposition. From 1615 there are records of regular payments for wine for the preachers. In his will of 1618 John Essome of Drayton, yeoman, left 10 shillings to the minister, Richard Marriatt, and 20 shillings to Daniel Wright, 'preacher of God's most holy word in Daventry'.[16] In 1632 the Borough Assembly Book stipulates that the lecture was to be kept on Wednesdays, which was market day. The sermon bell was to be rung at eight in the morning and, so that the fascinations of theology would not interfere with business, the proceedings were to be over by ten 'at the furthest'. Five years later Samuel Sutton, apothecary, left Mr. Timothy Dod 'ten shillings that he may preach at my funeral'. Calamy also mentions Robert Allen, vicar of Norton and of Adstone, as a popular preacher, 'one of the

lecturers at Daventry'. Allan was one of the ejected ministers of 1662.[17]

The greater part of the orders of 1607 set out the rules for the election of Bailiffs, burgesses, members of the commonalty and Recorders, but some notice of the way a dress-code was used to emphasise the dignity of those set in authority might be made. It was laid down that every Bailiff shall, in the year that he be Bailiff, 'be decently and comely apparreled according to the same manner which hath been used within the said borough heretofore, that is to say, his best gown to be of black cloth faced and welted with velvet, and made of the ancient fashion of citizen's gowns, and his best doublet of black satin, or of a satin of sad colour or of some other good black silk stuff fit for a magistrate to wear'. Newly appointed burgesses and twentymen were given one month to provide themselves with a gown, upon pain of 20 shillings for failing to do so. The whole company of burgesses and commonalty, 'decently apparreled in their best gowns', were required to be at the Bailiff's house at 8 o'clock in the morning on every fair day and feast day, and from thence to accompany him 'orderly two and two together' to the parish church. After service on fair days they were to accompany him to the reading of the proclamation about the said borough, 'and to bring the said bailiff home again unto his house according to the ancient custom'.

The remainder of the orders were chiefly concerned with the ways the craft companies conducted their business, and underlined how all this was sanctioned and controlled by the corporation. All that were made free by the crafts had to have their freedoms formalised by letters under the great seal of the borough. Some insight into the relative status of trades is shown by the fact that for every member of their company freed to work in Daventry mercers had to pay 20 shillings, for every member of the shoemakers 10 shillings, and for every of the carpenters and masons 5 shillings. Over the next century and more Daventry's leading citizens were nearly always mercers or drapers. All apprentices indentured in the borough had to be presented before the Bailiff and Recorder, and proper records of the start and completion of their apprenticeship kept in the book of the company. The last but one of these orders concerned restriction of entry into Daventry, only this time it concerned the poor. Inhabitants were forbidden to demise or let any cottage or tenement, or any part of a cottage or tenement, or take in as lodgers any strangers 'as are like to grow to be chargeable unto the said borough, if age, sickness, or impotencie shall come upon them', unless such inhabitants gave security to the corporation for such people and their dependants. Although it is hard to see quite how this control could have been exercised in the realities of life in the 17th century, it might have something to do with the fact that, at a time of a growing problem of poor relief in towns generally, Daventry never seemed to be over-exercised by the problem. There may be other reasons, such as the absence of records of the overseers of the poor but the impression is that, with a policy of prevention being better than cure, Daventry succeeded in keeping the poor at arms length. They had of course to go elsewhere.

No further constitutions were made until 1621, when new ones were added relating to fire fighting and prevention. All wells and pumps were to be put into good working order and a duty of provision of a leather bucket to be ready in case of fire was laid on a list of the inhabitants. Burgesses, as the wealthier sort, were to provide two buckets each. Another constitution made the common beadle responsible for ensuring that hogs were not allowed to wander the streets 'at the going afield or coming home of the hogherds'. Yet, it proved one thing to make new orders and quite another to see them carried out. A decade later the corporation were obliged to reiterate both orders. In the case of fire precautions, those responsible for two buckets were now required to provide ladders as well.

The finances of the borough were in the hands of the Bailiff, who had to submit his accounts quarterly. Daventry being a small place, these were relatively simple. The sources of income were quarterage money from the craft companies, freedom money from 'forreners', rents from a few houses and certain parcels of land controlled by the corporation and the profits of the two fairs. There was also the occasional legacy, such as that of Brian Abbey, who left £60 to the poor in 1630. In addition to miscellaneous payments, regular items of expenditure were the payment of wages to the sexton, the clerk and the molecatcher, and from 1602 the leasing of the manorial rights from the family who had

acquired them from the Duchy of Lancaster. In the Jacobean era there were regular New Year gifts of wine and sugar loaves to Sir Richard Knightley, and more occasional ones to locally influential people such as Lord Spencer, Sir Eusebie Andew and Mr. Raynsford, who became Recorder of Daventry on the death of Thomas Thornton. Wine was also provided for visiting preachers and for the entertaining of the judges in 1633 and 1636, when the assizes were held in Daventry instead of plague-affected Northampton. In 1616 there was a payment to the King's Players of 6s. 8d. Three years later 10 shillings was paid to the Prince's Players for performing in the town. Unfortunately, from 1624 such details cease to be available. From then on the Bailiffs' Accounts use the uninformative phrase 'as per bill of accounts'.

The local government of Daventry was shared between the corporation and the lord of the manor's court. The connection became more intimate from 1603 when the corporation acquired a lease of the manorial rights from Sir Moile Finch and his partner, Robert Lee, citizen and alderman of London, who had acquired them from Queen Elizabeth and the Duchy of Lancaster.[18] The first lease ran for 20 years and was regularly renewed thereafter. The two bodies worked closely together, decisions taken by the Bailiff and burgesses being carried out by the manor court, such as, for example, the above mentioned fire precautions or the letting of accommodation to poor strangers. The manorial court also took over the payment of town servants such as the moletaker. The main business of the manorial court was essentially the regulation of the farming of the open fields and commons, and adjudicating on disputes over such matters as paving, drainage, the removal of nuisances which annoyed neighbours or encroached on the 'lord's waste'. Decisions reached, and the 'paynes' for transgressing them, were duly recorded in the court leet book.[19] Alongside orders relating to such matters as the numbers of animals per farmer and cottager allowed grazing rights, pasturing, scouring ditches and payment of the molecatcher and the swineherds, it was decided (in 1607) that no one over 12 years or under 60 should have gleaning rights 'unless impotent or lame'. Houses 'that be no cottages and therefore have no Commons in the fields' were listed in 1604, over sixty of them, indicating how the number of new dwellings in Daventry had increased in the recent past.

Economic and social developments 1590 to 1676

It is difficult to arrive at reliable figures for the population for any time before the first national census in 1801, by which time Daventry had grown to 2,582. We know that in the 16th century the population generally was on the increase. By the time Queen Elizabeth ascended the throne, it had probably recovered the high point of the Middle Ages. If that is true for Daventry, then its population would have been around 1000. The next usable figure is that of the Compton religious census of 1676, which gives a figure for Daventry of 1,450 for 'persons young and old' plus eight 'obstinate separatists'. A calculation of the difference between baptisms and burials recorded in the parish registers between 1590 and 1675 supports the assumption of a town whose population was growing very slowly. Over these 86 years the excess of baptisms over burials amounted to no more than 430. The periods of greatest growth were the decades between 1600 to 1619 and 1630 to 1639. Looking at the statistics for this period what is most obvious is the heavy impact of mortality. The effect of plague and other contagions is shown by such years as 1597, when the excess of deaths over baptisms was 62, 1604 when it was 87, 1625 when it was 139 and 1642 when it was 69. The 1620s and the 1640s were decades when burials exceeded baptisms, the former by 92, the latter by 28. In the better remembered plague years of 1661-5 there was an excess of burials over baptisms each year, though the excess for 1665, the year of the Great Plague of London, was a mere 20. This may have been luck, but more likely it was the result of the severe plague orders issued by the county magistrates which closed the markets and threatened draconian punishments for anyone breaking the rules of quarantine.[20]

Daventry's economy rested on farming, its markets and fairs and the trades that served them, and business associated with wayfaring. All were inter-connected. Although numbers of farmers remained fairly constant, many tradesmen and inn-keepers had some land, and anyone who made money usually invested in land as the surest way of transmitting wealth to the next generation. The market flourished, becoming known as a specialist one for sheep and horses, and in 1656, with the purchase of the right to hold an extra one, Daventry's fairs increased to four. The history of the crafts in Daventry between 1590 and 1675 has been thoroughly researched by Mr. Davenport.[21] According to his calculations, in these years the Shoemakers' Company registered 259 freemen, the Mercers 215 and the Masons 117. These totals for 86 years of economic activity are rather on the modest size, partly because Daventry was a small market town serving its own restricted hinterland, recruiting most of its workforce locally, and because there was almost certainly certainly under-registration. Moreover, these registers did not list the journeymen (men who had completed their apprenticeships but who had not taken up their freedom) working in the town at any one time. The shoemakers embraced 24 trades, involving all those working leather and some in metal, the mercers embraced 20 trades, mainly mercers, drapers, haberdashers and tailors but also some in cloth production (though this was only on a very minor scale in 17th-century Daventry), apothecaries, barbers and some bakers and grocers. Generally, as we have seen, the victualling trades were excluded from the 1590 arrangements, but the bakers and grocers were allowed to keep their rights and remained in the company of mercers. The records contain lists of the companies in 1631 and 1676. The mercers had 29 and 46 freemen respectively, the shoemakers 31 and 76 and the masons 32 and 27. If the shoemakers were the most numerous amongst the crafts, the mercers were, as noted, the richest and the most important politically.

The companies kept registers of apprentices. Over the whole period the names of 365 apprentices are listed, 173 to the trades of the shoemakers, 119 to the mercers and 73 to the masons. Most came from within a 15-mile radius, though a few apprenticed to mercers came from further afield. Most served the customary seven to nine years with their masters, with whom they dwelt. Davenport examined the extent to which those out of their time took up their freedom in Daventry. The figure for the shoemakers and masons was 62 per cent, whilst that for the mercers was 51. There are only passing references to women in these records. Three widows took up their freedoms upon the deaths of their husbands and had sons apprenticed to them. No girls are recorded being bound apprentice, though in 1605 Christian Ollyver bound herself to a miller in Daventry for four years to be taught how to make bone lace by his wife. This was perhaps a poor law case rather than a normal apprenticeship.

As a market and road town Daventry was well known for its inns and alehouses. Shakespeare, in *Henry IV, Part I* refers to 'the red-nosed inkeeper of Daintree'. The urban inn played an important part in the business of inland trade in this period. Some catered for carriers and drovers, offering provision for the holding and feeding of cattle. In this period much trade migrated from the market place into the inns, and certain of them provided stores for produce and services for dealers buying produce for the London market. The inns also had administrative and political functions. When Ship Money was levied in the 1630s the constables of the parishes in Daventry's market area were ordered to pay in the tax money at the *Wheat Sheaf* on the specified date before eight in the morning. Inns also became centres of social life and entertainment, housing performing players, staging cock-fights and, in a more genteel era, adding assembly rooms for meetings, balls and musical performances. Innkeepers were often to be numbered amongst the ranks of the well-to-do, and had status accordingly. They were also mobile, moving from one town to another in the course of their working lives. The *Wheat Sheaf* is mentioned in the Dragge Book of 1571, and the *Saracen's Head* sometime not long after. In 1622 William Howse, citizen and apothecary of London, sold a messuage in Daventry 'heretofore called the *Keye* and now called the *Saracens Head*, late in the occupation of Margaret Bostocke widow mother of William Howse' to Henry Goosey and Isobell his wife and Richard Howse of London, haberdasher, for £120. Thirty-three years later, Richard Howse, gentleman, sold it on to John Wodell of Daventry, innkeeper, for £167.[22] Widows often carried on the businesses of their late husbands, and sometimes with style, as the Somerset gentleman Thomas Baskerville appreciated, when he visited Daventry in 1673: 'we lay at the Sign of the *Swan*, near the church, Mrs. Bostocke, a widow, a proper gentlewoman, the landlady of it … Formerly the wife of a handsome tall gentleman of that name'. It seems certain that our two Mrs. Bostockes married into the same family of Daventry innkeepers. It probably needed a different style to manage one of Daventry's alehouses, the *Kings Arms* mentioned in the will of Michael Warwick in 1618.[23]

In this period one family stands out very prominently, the Farmers, prosperous mercers and drapers, who frequently served as masters of that craft company and in other offices in the town. In the 65 years from 1576 they were Bailiffs of Daventry on no less than 17 occasions. In 1626, Edward Farmer served in that office and also on the corporation were Richard, John and Benjamin, who was warden of the mercers. Three years later, five Farmers were in the list of 24 well-to-do contributors to Charles I's Subsidy, and they paid over a third of the total sum raised. Farmers were Bailiffs in five of the ten years in the 1620s. The last of the third generation of the family to figure prominently was Edward Farmer, a capital burgess in the later 1640s and '50s. By 1649 the family had done so well out of mercery that they invested their wealth in property. Under the wills of his grandfather and father, Dutton Farmer and Richard Farmer, both deceased, Richard Farmer, 'an infant under twenty one', took over the tenancy of the Christ Church estate. Although this Richard died in 1662, the family remained the tenants of Christ Church until 1751, though they went off to live in Northampton. The last of the line to be tenant of the Daventry estate was Edward Farmer 'of London, gent'.[24]

Daventry and the Great Rebellion

In 1629, King Charles, having had enough of the religious and political opposition to his government, prorogued parliament, resolving to govern without it. This he did for 11 years. In order to raise revenues he adopted various policies which provoked discontent, the greatest arising out of Ship Money, raised to maintain and re-equip the navy. In 1635 the county of Northampton was assessed at £6,000 for the provision of a ship of war, Daventry's liability being £50. Although Daventry paid up without protest, the sheriff reported widespread opposition and obstruction from individuals in other places, local examples being Richard Robins in Long Buckby and Richard Smith in Newnham. In 1638 another £50 was laid upon the town and amongst the names of those opposed to the payment of this tax was Edward Farmer, quoted as saying that 'he had never paid the money he was taxed at and never would, and that it was a good deed to beat such drunken rascally rogues as they [the two collectors] were out of the town'. In December he was up before the law, forced to eat his words and pay. However, by 1639, the government were finding it harder and harder to collect this tax. The sheriff, Sir John Hanbury, informed the Council that Brackley would not pay its £50, and that he could not get to Northampton because of the plague there 'neither can I get any money in other towns without distraining, and into many towns my men dare not enter to distrain for fear of being killed; some of my best bailiffs have forsaken me and will not meddle any more in that service'. Shortly after warrants for the non-return of ship money were laid on the mayors of Northampton and Higham Ferrers and the Bailiff of Daventry.[25]

The King's 'eleven years tyranny' began to collapse in 1640 in the face of Scottish resistance to the re-introduction of the episcopate and the Prayer Book into that country. A Scottish army invaded England. At first the king hoped that patriotism would overcome the hostility that had built up against him. He was mistaken. In May Northamptonshire was required to raise trained bands to march against the Scots. The Eastern Division under the Earl of Exeter agreed to pay coat and conduct money, but the West refused, and the trained bands refused to be disciplined by, or to go with any other commanders than local ones. There was no stomach for a war against the Scots. In July, Sir Jacob Astley's regiment 'out of Berks and Oxon' mutinied when passing through Daventry. When parliament was called a petition from the freeholders of Northamptonshire summed up the feelings of those opposed to the king: 'That of late we have been unusually and insupportably charged, troubled and grieved in our consciences, persons, and estates by innovation in religion, exactions in spiritual courts, molestations of our most Godly and learned ministers, ship money, monopolies, undue impositions, army money, wagon money, horse money, conduct money, and enlarging the forest beyond the ancient bounds, and the like'.[26] They elected two puritan squires, John Crewe of Steane and Sir Gilbert Pickering of Titchmarsh. Within two years the king started a war against his subjects.

Because of its location on the roads from Oxford into the East Midlands and from London to the West Midlands and Chester, and because of the military geography of the conflict locally, Daventry could not be other than neutral in the Great Rebellion. Northampton came out strongly for the parliament, and local royalist places were soon captured. However, the king made Oxford his base and Banbury was its forward position.

Until 1646 it successfully resisted attacks from the enemy in Northampton. On the road to Banbury, soldiers of both sides passed though the town and saw Daventry as fair game for taxes and supplies. At the start of the war the Earl of Northampton seized carriers' horses from Chester in the Daventry area for the use of his troops at Banbury. After the battle of Cropredy in June 1644, Waller, the Parliamentary commander, retired with his troops to Daventry for over a week. In 1645 Charles I lodged at the *Wheat Sheaf* for five days before the battle of Naseby, his men camping on Borough Hill.

We know very little about Daventry in this era except that the Wars exacted a severe price on the town's economy. From 1640 to 1646 no records were entered in the Borough Assembly Book, or the Bailiffs' Accounts or the Manorial Court Book. Weekly markets went on, though probably on a reduced scale. The fairs probably did not and wayfaring must have been adversely affected. In addition these years saw severe outbreaks of contagion. It is likely that Daventry royalists left for Oxford, and that ardent supporters of the parliament gravitated to Northampton, though we have no real information on this. We do know that Edward Farmer Esq. sat on the Northamptonshire Committee for Sequestrations of Malignants' Estates in 1643, along with local squires such as Sir John Dryden, Sir Christopher Knightley and John Crewe. Their instructions were to seize all the property of bishops and other persons 'opposed to the parliamentary forces in any manner' and 'two parts' of all the property of 'all and every Papist'. Farmer and 'Mr. Barkley, Daventry' were Commissioners for Militia to Suppress Insurrections and Preserve the Peace for the Counties of Northampton and Rutland, which was set up in March 1655.[27] Henry Barkeley was on the corporation and had been Bailiff in 1648-9. No doubt by then most men on the corporation were supporters of the regime. One who was to play a part in the early history of Nonconformity was John Manley, Bailiff in 1654-5.

As in many parishes the church in Daventry came under persecution in the Civil War era, though the details are by no means all clear. In 1639 a Richard Farmer, probably the same person who was rector of Charwelton, was curate. Ten years later he died and was buried in Daventry, but was not curate when he died. In

1647 he had been replaced by Samuel Crofts, the son of the schoolmaster of Daventry. Crofts was a survivor. He came in, presumably as a Presbyterian, and was Cromwellian Register in 1653, but because he took the oath demanded by the Act of Uniformity in 1662, and because the man he replaced was long dead, he held on to the living after the Restoration, dying in harness in 1666. During his incumbency, Timothy Dod, son of John Dod of Fawsley, was appointed afternoon lecturer, for which a salary of £40 a year, equal to the estimated value of Crofts' living, was paid him by the inhabitants of Daventry. He was a popular preacher, but towards the close of his ministry became so corpulent that he could not squeeze into the pulpit, and was obliged to officiate in a pew. Refusing to take the oath in 1662, he retired to private life and was much respected, being of an humble affable disposition, 'though tinctured with melancholy'.[28] At that time fat men were often respected, being viewed as 'prodigies of nature', but the Restoration made all puritans melancholy. Dod died in Everdon in 1665, whence he had gone to escape the plague.

After Cromwell's death in 1658 the constitution of the Commonwealth became harder to work. Richard Cromwell was not a chip off the old block. General Monck and elements in the army determined on a restoration of the monarchy, though not on terms Charles I would have accepted. For royalists and churchmen, who had suffered their version of 'eleven years tyranny', the world was to be 'turned the right way up' again. For republicans such as General Lambert this was too much. He rebelled, and made his last stand just outside Daventry. The Church of England was also restored to its position as the official religion of the state. An Act of Uniformity was passed. Clergymen, academics and teachers were given until 24 August 1662, St Bartholomew's day, to take the oath the Act demanded. Those who refused were cast out. As we have seen, Crofts took the oath and remained perpetual curate in Daventry to the end of his days.

The restoration of the monarchy and the Established Church in the 1660s marks the beginning of a new era in Daventry, as elsewhere. It began with religious, political and social divisions, painful to the losers, not to mention the threat of another terrifying visitation of the plague. In the longer term 'the long 18th century' was to prove one of the most prosperous and successful periods in the town's history.

Six

'A Town of Very Good Business': Later Stuart and Georgian Daventry

Nonconformity 1662 to 1790

The Act of Uniformity was one of a series of laws designed to crush Dissent, or, if that was impossible, consign it to the margins of English life. The first was the Corporation Act of 1661, by which all magistrates were required to take the Sacrament according to the rites of the Church of England. This, in Daventry, as in most other boroughs, made it impossible for Dissenters to become burgesses from then on. Down to 1835 the corporation was entirely identified with Toryism and the Church. Eventually abandoned by the rural gentry and the well-to-do town burgesses who had been such influential supporters of the puritan movement for close on a century, after 1662 Dissent became a lower-class thing than before. A third enactment which affected Nonconformists was the Conventicle Act of 1664, which forbade more than five persons to assemble at meetings (conventicles) in private households. This was complemented by the Five Mile Act (1665) which required all ministers who had not subscribed to the Act of Uniformity to take an oath of non-resistance, swearing never to attempt any change in church or state. It prohibited all who refused, as most did, from coming within five miles of any incorporated town, or any place where they had been ministers. This had the effect of scattering ejected ministers, though clandestinely they continued to visit places where they had supporters. These Acts (the so-called 'Clarendon Code') were passed at a time of strong Anglican reaction. Their effectiveness was reduced by the fact that they could not be strictly enforced, that many in authority preferred toleration, and perhaps most of all by the obstinate refusal of Dissenters to be suppressed. Nevertheless, the persecution they underwent was real and generally successful in keeping their numbers to a minimum.

Old established Dissenting congregations usually date their origins from one of three dates, 1662, the year of the great ejection, 1672, when, under Charles II's Declaration of Indulgence, Nonconformists were given freedom of worship provided they registered their meeting houses, or 1689, when they were able to come into the open under William III's Act of Toleration. As there was no ejected minister to rally round in Daventry, it is to the years after 1662 that we must look for the start of Nonconformity. The first meetings of Dissenters were held at night in the house in Drayton of John Manley, a former Bailiff, which backed on to the fields and facilitated a quick exit in case of detection. The authorities were aware of these meetings, as Archdeacon Palmer made clear in 1669:

> Here are frequent Conventicles, but not fixed. Sometimes 2 or 3 a month, sometimes as many in a week as the preachers happen to come. They meet at Mr. John Manley's to the number of 20, 40 and 60, most women. Not above 6 of them forsake the Church. Their teachers non-conformists who pretend to be journeying upon that road.[1]

At the time of the Declaration of Indulgence, when the penal laws were temporarily suspended and licences granted, James Cave, a Banbury man who had been a captain in the wars in Scotland, and then minister at Crosthwaite in Cumberland, and Daniel Williams, later a leading London minister, were licensed as teachers, and the houses of Widow Manley, James Cave and Allen Linzey as meeting places. The latter had been landlord of the *Swan*, one of the foremost inns in the town, and had been converted by a travelling preacher who lodged there during an illness. Part of his property in High Street was turned into a meeting house, the original place of worship of the Daventry Dissenters. Linzey died before he could lease it to them formally, but in his will of

23 The Dissenting chapel, set discreetly in a yard off Sheaf Street (L.G. Tooby).

1694 declared that it was his wish 'that the meeting house shall be continued to the same use as it is now'.[2] And it was, until a new one was built in 1722.

The Declaration of Indulgence was soon revoked. Persecution resumed, but the survival of Nonconformity was made possible by the Toleration Act of 1689. Except for the names of some preachers, little is known of the early years of the Daventry congregation, except that it was small and originally Presbyterian. In 1664 Richard Martyn, ejected vicar of Monks Kirby in Warwickshire, said to be 'of Daventry', preached in Southam. James Cave, after quitting Crosthwaite, 'remov'd often from one Place to another, till marrying at Daventry in Northamptonshire, he settl'd there and contin'd there till he came to London'. As we have seen, he was licensed to preach at his house in 1672. In the 1690s John Worth, formerly minister at Kilsby and preacher at Weedon Bec, was in the town, as was Andrew Barnett, ejected minister of Rodington, Salop, whose sermon on the death of Queen Mary was printed in Daventry in 1694.[3] Then followed the short pastorates of Thomas Havell, John Mason and John Cambden and a Mr. Jolly.

It seems, however, that the cause was given a firm foundation in the pastorate of Daniel Mattock, who succeeded Jolly in 1720. About this time the congregation became Independent. The minister, who stayed until 1736, was an able preacher, and this, and the effect of the lifting of penalties for non-attendance at church, meant a growing congregation. The old meeting house became too small. In 1721 a house in Sheaf Street, with land adjoining, was bought and the present chapel erected a year later. Located discreetly in a court-yard off the street, internally it is a preaching box, intimate and austere. It is hard to ascertain how many adherents the Independents had at any particular time in the 18th century, but they were never numerous. Its trustees and deacons were the middling sort—yeomen, graziers, maltsters, grocers, bakers, wheelwrights. Much of their non-religious as well as their religious

24 Dated downspout, Independent chapel (L.G. Tooby).

activities centred on the chapel, and at this time they were remarkably self-contained and inward-looking. By the later part of the century they had a network of charities, the earliest of which was Mary Hill's bequest of 1731 of 20 shillings per annum to be distributed amongst the poor of the congregation. Others were left for the upkeep of the buildings, the support of the minister and the running of a school, which was still in existence in 1820, when it advertised for a master. The next information we have of a Protestant Dissenters' school is the British School of 1842, whose records make no mention of its predecessor.[4]

By about 1750 the Independents of North-amptonshire were in good shape, their leaders prospering in their trades, their ablest pastors men of some learning. When the Dissenting

25   The Dissenting Academy Building, 1974.

Academy formerly located in Northampton moved to Daventry in 1752, for almost four decades the town became the intellectual centre of Nonconformity in this part of the Midlands. In the 18th century the English universities were closed to Dissenters and academies were founded to provide a higher education for their sons, especially for those wishing to train for the ministry. The best known in the Midlands was that run by the Rev. Philip Doddridge, minister of Castle Hill Independent chapel in Northampton. By 1751, when he died, the academy had established a high reputation, and more than two hundred students had studied there, including its next principal, Caleb Ashworth. At the time of Doddridge's death Ashworth was minister of Daventry chapel, but, despite Doddridge's recommendation in his last will and testament that Ashworth should succeed him, the Castle Hill congregation, exhibiting the God-given right of Dissenters to be obstinate, failed to agree to this, so the academy moved to Daventry.[5]

Like Doddridge, Ashworth was a Doctor of Divinity at a Scottish University, and an able and scholarly man. His 29-year pastorate was one of the great periods of nonconformity in the town and was long remembered. The congregation responded to preachers of the calibre of Ashworth and his assistants. Ashworth's students came from as far afield as Lancashire, Yorkshire, Shropshire, Somerset and Suffolk, entering the academy at fifteen, studying for three or four years, and then returning to their native places or to a chapel ministry. It is said that in the 37 years of its existence Daventry academy sent forth nearly another 300 ministers, perhaps the best known being Joseph Priestley, celebrated as a theologian, scientist and Radical, who was to pay for his initial enthusiasm for the French Revolution. Notable local men included William Field of Warwick (the great grandson of Oliver Cromwell) and the Rev. Thomas Northcote Toller, minister at Kettering for over fifty years. The intellectual standard under Ashworth was high, but the place obtained some odium among the stricter

Nonconformists in his time because a number of his pupils moved towards Unitarianism. Ashworth's teaching methods were blamed, perhaps unjustly, for this.[6]

Ashworth's successor in 1775 was another pupil of Doddridge's, Thomas Robins. He is said to have been a man of greater ability than Ashworth, and an extremely fine preacher, but after only six years at the academy he strained his voice after preaching three times in one day at Kettering, and it never recovered enough to allow him to resume the ministry. He lived until 1810 making a poor living as a bookseller. His successor was Thomas Belsham. When he accepted the post he was still orthodox, but he became dissatisfied with the doctrine of the Trinity whilst principal of Daventry. In 1789 he was forced to resign, and the academy moved back to Northampton. Although the congregation was well-established and even flourishing, harmony in all Dissenting chapels depended not only on the vigour and intellectual development of the minister but his ability to carry his people with him. The Daventry congregation would not tolerate being taken too far towards unorthodoxy. Belsham was succeeded by the Rev. T. Willis Paterson (1789-96), a former student of the academy who was orthodox, and he by the John Morell, who was not. Within two years, Morell had embraced Unitarian ideas and departed.[7]

The particular character of Daventry's Nonconformity was shaped by the fact that no other chapels ever established themselves there, until the Wesleyans arrived. Baptists or Quakers never put down roots. In the early 18th century one or two 'anabaptists' occasionally antagonised the curate over baptismal and burial matters but there were never enough to form a congregation. In religion, as in other ways, Daventry was not a complex place: in the century following the Glorious Revolution its religious pattern could not have been simpler. It had one church and one Nonconformist meeting house.

The Church in Daventry

The Anglican incumbent of Daventry, as we have seen, was neither rector nor vicar. His title was the unsatisfactory and legally uncertain one of perpetual curate, an 'inferior' title not abolished in the Church of England until 1868. Perpetual curacies were attached either to district churches, or to impropriate or appropriate rectories. The

curacy of Daventry was of the latter kind and, as we have seen, its origins went back to the arrangements made by the Priory in the Middle Ages. After the Daventry possessions of the Priory passed to Christ Church in Oxford, the college became patron of the living, but the parsonage was one of these properties leased out to the college's tenant, and he in turn had to find a curate. The farming of the living was still being practised in 1630, though for a time in that decade the college seems to have taken a more direct interest in the living than hitherto. If so, it was short-lived. In the Civil War local connections rather than the patronage of royalist Christ Church were more important to curates of Daventry. Certainly Crofts owed his preferment to local influences.

After the Restoration Crofts must have been happier than before. He no longer had to share his church with Preacher Dod, and his stipend was enhanced. In his will of 1662, Richard Farmer made arrangements for his heirs to pay an annual bequest to the curate arising out of their income from the tenancy of the Christ Church property, to which was added another £6 for the rent of a house. The following year Crofts made an agreement with the Bailiff and burgesses that, in return for surrendering the mastership of the Grammar School, they would pay him £30 a

26 Parish church. Silver communion plate, inscribed 'The Gift of Edward Farmer Gentleman for the use of the Parish Church of Daventree 1640 and Enlarg'd by the Same Parish 1716'.

year, for which he undertook to preach twice in the parish church on the Lord's day.[8] The improving of his position and these modest pay rises may have pleased Crofts, but his successors made their dissatisfaction with the living and its duties very clear in the Daventry Tithing Book, in which several of them, from the late 1690s to 1818, left notes for the guidance of their successors.[9] The first entry, made by Charles Allestree, curate 1687 to 1707, sets the tone. It declares roundly: 'The trouble and duty of exercising the ministerial function at Daventry is very great and discouraging and every man will find it so upon trial'. By the standards of the time it seems the workload of the minister of Daventry was heavy. The weight was felt to be the more burdensome, one suspects, because the stipend was so poor and the status so inferior in a borough where status meant much. Although it grew under Allestree, in the first half of the 18th century the stipend never seems to have exceeded £120, little enough on which to have employed a curate, and certainly not sufficient to live well. And there was not even a house.

Crofts' successor was John Frauncis, who, despite an incumbency of 20 years, remains an obscure figure. All we know is that he graduated from Christ Church and that he was curate from 1667 to 1687. His successor, Charles Allestree, was rather different. His trenchant memoranda open the Tithing Book and record some early exchanges in the long battle to improve the living. Allestree was a new type. Socially better connected than his predecessors, he was sharper in asserting his rights, and expected his patrons in Oxford to support him. In the manner of the times, it was to the practice of pluralism that he and his successors turned as a way of improving their livings. In 1685 the college presented him to the living of Cassington, near Woodstock, and two years later to the curacy of Daventry. His first battle, which he won, was over the non-payment of tithes from certain farmers. He notes:

> I have rescued sixteen yard land from the power of an oppressor and made them tytheable as well as other parts of the field. And this matter is now inserted also into Mr. Farmers lease for the prevention of any encroachment for the future. So that now the minister has a right to all small tythes that arise in the parish and no body starts any pretended privilege or exemption.

Allestree also itemised other concessions he had secured in matters of fee and tax liabilities.[10]

Allestree's successor, Samuel Hartman, curate from 1707 to 1716, was also vicar of Badby. The son of a German protestant émigré from the kingdom of Poland, he was a graduate and petty canon of Christ Church, but the only reference to him in the Tithing Book is a dismissive note that 'he left only some confused papers which were of no use'. The writer was William Tayler, minister for the next 34 years. For much of his life in Daventry, as well as being minister, he was, like some before him, master of the Free Grammar School, endowed with £20 a year. Taylor also followed the paths of pluralism, being in succession vicar of Staverton (1723-26), vicar of Long Buckby (1730-38) and from 1728 rector of Malpas in Cheshire. The latter brought him to green pastures and he gave up the Grammar School in 1732. By then he had a curate. It is to Tayler that we owe the compilation of the Tithing Book in its present form. Into it he copied Allestree's notes, adding others of his own on a variety of matters. No other contributor reveals as much about clerical life in 18th-century Daventry.

The minister's stipend derived from a variety of sources and the Tithing Book makes it clear he had to be forever on the alert to see that he received his dues from all of them. The most stable part of his income—amounting to about a quarter—came from small tithes. These fell into two categories: 'compounded tithes' and tithes in kind. About 1700, in Allestree's time, an arrangement had been reached with the farmers of the parish that they should compound with the minister for their tithes at the rate of eight shillings to the yardland, a sum which became fixed by custom and never varied as long as tithes were paid. Tithes in kind consisted of tithes of the sheep which grazed on the common on Borough Hill, a hundred eggs at Easter, a tithe of pigs, a payment made by the owners of gardens and orchards, and a charge arising out of the town bakehouse and malt mill. Each year these had to be collected by the parson, and the issue was always contentious. Unless they wanted to lose income, the clergy had to be hard-nosed about their rights, a criterion Allestree and Tayler clearly fulfilled. Before 1753 (when Drayton was enclosed) compounded tithes brought in an income of just over £32 a year. From tithes in kind, not only was the income very small (at most £6 a year), it was more difficult to collect than compounded tithes. For instance, although the curate had the tithe of sheep on Borough Hill, by tradition it was limited to those grazing there on New Year's Day. According to Tayler, it was usual for the farmers to defraud him 'by some driving off their sheep and on a little before or after this time'.[11]

Another source of income was 'benefactions'. The principle one was the Farmer bequest of £26 a year already referred to; a second was a legacy of £1 in the will of Edward Sawbridge in 1722 for an annual sermon on Good Friday. A third source was Easter offerings and what the minister referred to in his accounts as 'contributions' or 'subscriptions'. The former were Easter payments of three pence per house (though some gave more). Besides Easter offerings there were also the quarterly contributions or subscriptions. Sometime between that date and 1751 this system was replaced by payments made by the parish for a sermon on Sunday afternoons, which in the second half of the century brought in between £20 and £25 a year. Finally there were a variety of payments received from small rents and 'surplice fees'. Each year the minister let the churchyard for grazing, and he also received 6s. 8d. for keeping the register. He received payment for weddings, banns, funerals, churchings and mortuaries, the latter often in the form of silk hat-bands and gloves. In total, these surplice

27   The new church of Holy Cross.

fees and small rents could range from as low as £7 or £8 a year in the early part of the century, to as high as £31 in 1788.

In 1750 Tayler was succeeded by James Affleck, who also served 34 years. The sixth son of a country gentleman, his mother was a niece of Sir Gilbert Dolben, Bart., of Finedon, and two of his sons succeeded in turn to a baronetcy. In 1757 he was presented to the living of Finedon, and thereafter employed a curate in Daventry. In his time two events of considerable local importance happened. In 1751-53 Drayton field was enclosed and he and his successors became the possessors of an estate there in lieu of their extinguished tithe rights. This produced a rental which increased in a very satisfactory manner as the century wore on and was a major factor in the enhancement of the living. The other was the complete rebuilding of the parish church.

By 1752 it had become clear that the fabric of the old church had decayed so much that it was becoming dangerous to continue using it for public worship. The parish took the decision to rebuild, the cost to be defrayed by public subscription. By the time a petition for a faculty had been presented to the bishop, they had raised £1,800. A commission was appointed to consider the application and was soon persuaded of the need for a new church. The episcopal seal was duly fixed to a faculty and the building work was entrusted to William Hiorne (or Hiorns) who, with his brother David, was then the leading mason in Warwick.[12] The work took six years. With a tower modelled, it is said, on that of St Giles-in-the-Fields in London, the new Holy Cross is that rarity in Northamptonshire, a fine 18th-century town church built in the classical manner. Set at the top of the market hill it is the focal point of a pleasing piece of townscape, a lasting reminder of the time when Daventry was a town of very good business.

The new church cost £3,468, considerably more than the sum estimated in the faculty. This was raised without difficulty by local subscription. In the old church many of the sittings were appropriated, and in the new church this principle was not abandoned, though clearly another method of apportionment to the traditional one of seats being attached to particular houses in the town had to be adopted. This was decided on at a parish meeting in late 1754, and approved by a faculty in the Consistory Court. Pews and seats in the new church were to be allotted according to the amount

28 Holy Cross, interior, the north gallery, from the east.

29 Glass panels in Holy Cross. *Left*, the arms of Christ Church, Oxford, *right*, the arms of the Earl of Wichilsea (L.G. Tooby).

subscribers had contributed to the cost of the re-building. There were, in addition, appropriated sittings for servants.[13] Once again their number varied according to size of subscription. The internal arrangements of the new church were simple and elegant. Basically a rectangular box, with a chancel, it has north, south and west galleries, below which are north and south aisles. In the centre of the church is the middle aisle divided into north and south sides. Despite having first choice of the gallery, the town notables chose front pews in the middle aisle. There, in a phalanx behind the corporation seats, were the leading burgesses, farmers and innkeepers and their families. In first place was the pew of Edward Sawbridge, draper, a £50 man, with three seats for his servants in the gallery behind. Sawbridge was church-warden, and Bailiff in 1753-4. After the deaths of all the original subscribers, their appropriated seats went with their houses, a reversion to the old system. Not all seats were appropriated. The faculty allotted a maximum of 450 for subscribers and their servants, 'reserving for the publick upwards of four hundred places more'. The latter had a choice of the less eligible seats in the aisles and galleries.

Education in Daventry 1660-1790

The Church reinforced its supremacy through the provision of schools. The fortunes of the older Free Grammar School were intimately bound up with the Church. It has been said that the school 'seems to have spent the larger portion of its existence in a state of suspended animation'. Perhaps that was because the objectives of the founder were not what was ever really wanted of a school by the parents of local boys. In reality the mastership became the first step on the ladder of preferment for young clergymen who acted as the minister's assistant, a first post for a career school master who moved on at the earliest op-portunity, or a sinecure for pluralists. The career of the Rev. John Cadman, master 1732 to 1762, illustrates two of these criteria. Six years after his appointment his stipend was augmented under the Farrer bequest, made in 1729 with the inten-tion of paying the schoolmaster, if he was in holy orders, to relieve the minister from some of the duties of his office. This money was used to purchase the first property at Cosford, added to a few years later by the English Charity school bequests. In 1749 Cadman's prospects were trans-formed when he was presented to the living of Whilton, which did not entail any need to move from Daventry. He continued to hold the mastership of the school for another 13 years.[14] In the 1760s the stipend of the master was advanced by the income from bequests made by John Sawbridge and his brother Edward, which at first were used towards the buying of a house

30   Postcard of *c.*1900 showing the market place and Holy Cross. In the foreground is Jesson's pump.

for the master in 1768, though later it was sold and the proceeds invested in consols. Between 1662 and 1787 there were 17 masters of the Free Grammar School and there were also times when there seems to have been no master at all.[15] It seems entirely possible that this did little damage to educational provision in the town. The real purpose of the position had long been diverted to provide for an assistant for the minister. From 1787 there were attempts to revitalise and modernise the Grammar School, but until the later 19th century progress on that front was rarely long-lasting.

So how and where did the children of the better-off and the middling sort receive an education? The former often educated their sons with tutors, usually clergymen, and then maybe sent them off to Rugby or some other private school. The sons of shopkeepers and small masters went to local private schools, having their education completed in the course of their apprenticeship, which in the case of retailers such as mercers, drapers and stationers was often in other market towns. Some may well have attended the private

schools for 'young gentlemen' started in Daventry, as in most other market towns, from about the middle of the century, though as these were set up to attract boarders, local boys may well have been in a minority. One such was the school started by Titus Wadsworth, a land surveyor, in 1773. His pupils were taught Latin, Greek, English Grammar, writing, arithmetic, keeping accounts and land surveying. It was still going on 23 years later, but which time Wadsworth had become a prominent burgess, serving his year as Bailiff in 1788-9.[16] In 1801 Thomas Sanders moved his Academy from Northampton, announcing that young gentlemen would be prepared for 'Trade, Counting House, Army, Navy, etc'. Forty years later it was still in existence, and by then Sanders' son, a Cambridge graduate, had become master of the Free Grammar School, to launch him on his way in the church, and his sisters were also in the private school business. Sanders also got on to the Corporation and served his time as Bailiff.[17] Daventry was home to boarding schools for young ladies, one of the earliest being that opened by a Miss Walker in the 1740s, and for another century or so there were always such establishments in the town. In 1769 Miss Scriven and her daughters announced their move from Northampton. Their pupils were taught needlework, given instruction in polite behaviour, and masters were engaged to teach music, dancing, French, and writing. Mrs. Scrivens' daughters carried on after their mother, and were still there in 1796.[18] Again, it is not certain how many of their young ladies came from the town itself: probably few.

In 1710 a number of Daventry people drew up Articles of Agreement for the opening of a charity school. These declared that 'profaneness and irreligion were greatly owing to the gross ignorance of the principles of Christianity, especially among the poorer sort' and that many of the poor were unable to afford for their children 'a christian and useful education nor to breed them up to any honest calling', and a number of subscribers agreed to contribute yearly towards the building and maintaining of a school for boys. This was the 'English Charity School'. The articles stated that not only were the boys to be taught to read, write and cast accounts, but were to be instructed in the knowledge and practice of the Church of England. The earliest records of the school date from 1722. In it some 24 boys and (from 1731) six girls, entering between the ages of seven and eleven, were educated. As well as being taught they were provided with a new set of clothing each year, though not for everyday use: a man was paid for handing out coats and caps to the boys as they assembled to go to church and collecting them afterwards. At the end of their school days the boys were apprenticed to a trade at the expense of the trustees.[19]

One of the problems of charities is that whilst initial subscribers can usually be found, persuading people to contribute year in year out is more difficult. The accounts show that within a few years the number of subscribers was on the decline. However, beginning with a modest bequest of £10 from William Sawbridge in 1719 followed by others from Dr. Maynard, Mrs. Combes and John Farrar, the charity was able to buy land at Cosford, the rents from which were sufficient to maintain the school well into modern times. In 1848 the Cosford estate was exchanged for one in Woodford, near Thrapston and the master had his salary augmented out of the Boddington estate purchased with the bequest of Edward Sawbridge in 1772.[20] There is a tradition that the school first assembled in a room at the Grammar School, but it soon moved to the old Priory building and there it stayed until rehoused in 1826 in a new building erected close by. It should be noted that new pupils were admitted by one way only—on the recommendation of one of the trustees. In the century after the Restoration children not able to secure a place in the English School or the Dissenters' School received whatever education they got beyond their mother's knee in Dame schools or such other 'private adventure schools' as existed in Daventry, schools which leave few records of their existence. Sunday Schools did not come into existence until the end of the 18th century.

Local Government

In 1675 the corporation surrendered its charter to King Charles II, who granted a new one. Most corporations did this after the Restoration. However, in Daventry the reasons for this seem to go back to a dispute in 1655 between the Bailiff and burgesses and the Shoemakers' Company, who had made one Richard Clifford of Northampton a freeman, in breach of the constitutions. For his refusal to appear before the Bailiff one of those involved was expelled as a burgess. Two years later it was resolved at a public meeting that the charter should be renewed as soon as convenient. In fact it took another eight years, and was seen through by the efforts of the new Recorder, William Buckby (who had succeeded his father-in-law, Sir Nicholas Raynsford, in 1667), and the good offices of Sir Heneage Finch, the Attorney General, who also happened to be lord of the manor of Daventry.[21]

The changes brought about by the new charter were important, if not numerous. The number of burgesses were reduced from 14 to 12. New officers, a chamberlain and two wardens, were to be appointed. These related to a major new development, the abolition of the craft companies. The right to grant freedoms and to enrol apprentices was now vested in the Bailiff, burgesses, chamberlain and wardens, the latter three being made responsible for the collection of entry fines. Trading and production were still confined to freemen and apprentices except for market and fair days. Why the abolition of the companies of craftsmen came about is not altogether clear. Most likely it reflected the determination of the corporation to have greater

31 Portrait of Charles II in the first letter of his charter of 1675.

1675. There was a new regulation regarding the election of the Bailiff. Instead of the burgesses and commonalty being involved in the nomination, from now on the Bailiff and burgesses would nominate two burgesses from whom the commonalty would choose one to be the next Bailiff. A similar process was to be followed for the nomination of the chamberlain, also elected yearly. The charter also laid it down that a house of correction was to be erected and a governor appointed. The liberties of the borough were to be extended throughout the whole parish, which meant that for the first time Drayton was incorporated into the borough. William Buckby, Esq. was appointed Recorder for life and Edward Bromwich, the Deputy-recorder was also to be Clerk of the Peace, a position which evolved into that of Town Clerk.

The Borough Assembly Book lists the names of all the freemen of Daventry in April 1676. The 12 burgesses head the list, all with 'gent.' after their names, then the freemen in the town, some 100 in number, followed by the names of 42 'Countrey men'. The callings of the burgess élite were still those that had dominated the corporation for the past century. Four (including John Willington, the Bailiff) were drapers and the ex-Bailiff was a mercer, two were shoemakers, two ironmongers, and there was one currier, one grocer and an apothecary. Looking at their assessments in the Hearth tax for 1670, three of the drapers and the mercer had houses assessed as having the greatest number of hearths (six). The rest of the burgesses had three- to five-hearth houses, whilst, typically, ordinary freemen occupied in the main one-, two- or three-hearth dwellings.[22]

32 Sir Heneage Finch, created Baron Finch of Daventry when Attorney General to King Charles II and Lord Keeper of the Great Seal. Evelyn styled him 'the smooth-tongued solicitor'.

control of freedoms and apprenticeships and the income they produced. It perhaps reflected the spirit of the time, when, with Crown approval, the powers of town authorities were tightened.

There is no record of any burgess of Daventry being purged for activities in the Civil War or under the Commonwealth, as happened elsewhere. Nonetheless it was felt necessary to have guarantees in the charter that no proceedings would be started by the government for 'any offences or usurpation done or committed' before

The burgesses of Daventry were acutely conscious of their status. The visible symbols of the authority of the corporation were the maces, and,

33 The lesser mace of Daventry corporation.

after the renewal of the charter, the old great mace was exchanged for a new one bearing the arms of Charles II. The lesser mace was replaced in 1722.[23] These symbols of civic authority were borne by two sergeants-at-mace, who wore black gowns of 'German serge'. The town crier, too, wore a livery coat of red cloth. The most regular public display of the civic authority continued to be when the members of the corporation processed on Sundays and feast days, and on market and fair days.

In this period, certain families were prominent as burgesses over several generations, and proved generous to the place where they lived, moved and made their fortunes. One such were the Sawbridges, drapers by trade. The first to be connected with Daventry was William Sawbridge (1650-1719), whose forbears came from Hillmorton in Warwickshire.[24] He came to Daventry in 1665 to be apprenticed to a draper for nine years. In 1675, out of his time, he took up his freedom and went into business on his own, and was straight away elected to the ranks of the commonalty. In 1686 he was made burgess, and was Bailiff four times. His will of 1718 reveals him to have been a man of some wealth, civic pride and charitable instincts. In addition to bequests to his family, he left £5 to be

34   The head of the lesser mace.

35   Edward Sawbridge's confirmation of the investment of the bequest of John Watters, 1763.

distributed among the poor of Daventry in six-pound loaves, and £10 to the charity school, the interest thereof to be used for the apprenticing of one poor boy a year to a trade, 'but if such school should cease, or come to nothing, the said ten pounds to be for teaching three poor children for ever to read'.

His three sons who survived childhood were each in turn apprenticed to their father to learn the drapery business. Two stayed in Daventry but never married, while the third moved to London. Of the three, it was Edward Sawbridge (1682-1775), who played the more prominent part in the public life of the town. He was made burgess in 1708 and, like his father before him, was four times Bailiff. It was he who presented the town with a new lesser mace in 1722. In his will he left £1,400 to be laid out in land upon trust, to pay the following sums annually: £8 to the Bailiff to be used towards paying salaries and wages of town servants and officers—the Recorder, the town clerk, the two sergeants at mace, and the minister and his successors to preach a sermon on Good Friday. Ten pounds a year was to be used each year for apprenticing the son of 'an honest poor person of the parish' to trade, the master of the English Charity school was to have his salary augmented by £4 a year, the present Bailiff was to have 20 shillings 'for his trouble about the trusts of the will', and the residue, after deducting expenses, was to be distributed on the feast of St Paul amongst the poorest persons in the parish. This £1,400, together with £100 from Walford's charity, went on the purchase of the land at Boddington, the rents thereof to be used to meet Sawbridge's bequests and the relief of the poor.[25]

His brother John played less of a part in public life. He was made burgess in 1715, but resigned four years later to devote himself to business. Nevertheless, when he died in 1743 amongst his bequests was £150 towards buying a house for the master of the Grammar school, a post which his sister Dorothy's husband, the Rev. William Collier, once held. Further Sawbridge concern for Daventry was expressed in the will of another of his sisters, Frances Thompson, who left £100 the interest on which was to be distributed annually to 15 poor widows. Their brother William, who moved to London, married into a family with considerable property in Hackney. His son, Henry (1719-1807), born in the parish of St Lawrence

Jewry in London, retired to Northamptonshire to an estate he bought in East Haddon. Thus another grandson of a Daventry draper joined the ranks of landowners. The Sawbridge connection with Daventry was maintained through Henry's grandson, Henry Barne Sawbridge, who was Recorder from 1803 to 1821.

In the Georgian era professional men were attracted to Daventry and in the course of time some, notably the surgeons, became burgesses. It was not necessary for surgeons to take up their freedom, though their predecessors, apothecaries and barbers, did. The most prominent of this class of medical burgesses were the Wildgooses. The first was Charles Wildgoose, surgeon and apothecary, who was elected a burgess in 1736, the year his son John was apprenticed to him for seven years. Charles Wildgoose became Bailiff the following year and the connection with the corporation was maintained through three more generations down to 1839, when Robert Wildgoose, his great grandson, died, having served twice as Bailiff and once as Daventry's Mayor. In the last year of the old corporation, 1835, three of the 12 burgesses were medical men.

Down to 1835 the corporation continued to exercise the functions allotted to it under its charter—the regulation of the markets and fairs, the registering of freemen and apprentices, the running of certain charities, the letting of certain properties and the administration of Justices' justice. These were reflected in an inventory of the moveable property of the borough handed over in November 1717 to William Sawbridge, the incoming Bailiff. It consisted of 23 volumes of Acts of Parliament, 'twenty three books more', two maces and a case, two black boxes 'with leases and other writings in them belonging to the Poores Closes', one 'Pazboard box empty', and a range of measures for use in the market and fairs. These included a one yard and a one ell measure, two brass quarts, one pewter quart and two brass pints, scales, boxes of weights, one brass strike (for the measurement of grain), one wooden strike, a wooden peck, and (for liquid measurement) a wooden gallon, half gallon and quarter gallon. These are preserved in the Daventry and District Museum. In addition to organising rudimentary fire-fighting precautions (the inventory also included 11 leather buckets), and the administration of the charities, the Bailiff, ex-Bailiff and the Recorder, or his deputy, were responsible for the keeping of the peace in the borough. Sessions of the Peace at which the Recorder attended were held once a year. They seem to have had little to do. The 1835 Royal Commission on Municipal Corporations noted that 'trifling cases only are tried. One felony on an average is said to be tried in every five years; scarcely one misdemeanour on an average is said to be tried at each sessions'.[26] There were, of course, times when the magistrates were faced with alarming little local difficulties. The Borough Assembly Book has a memorandum of 1677 to prosecute those 'as have been guilty of abetting those persons that did concerne them-selves in playing footeball or in the Mutony or disturbance that did arise therefrom'.[27] The Royal Commission also noted that there was formerly a Court of Record for the recovery of debts above 40 shillings and under £100, but by 1835 it had fallen into disuse.

For much of the 18th century the pattern and scale of the corporation's business changed little. The Borough Assembly Book records little more than the formalities of appointing a new Bailiff each year and the more infrequent appointments, resignations and replacements of burgesses, commonalty, Recorders, Deputy Recorders and masters of the Free Grammar School. Its powers fixed by charter, Daventry's corporation was the happy prisoner of history and, because this was England, where the older an institution becomes the more it is venerated, its members gloried in their status and position. The pleasures of being big fish in a small pond should never be under-estimated.

Sharing in the local government of the town was the lord of the manor through his manorial court. Down to 1786 the lordship remained in the hands of the Finch family, Barons of Daventry and subsequently Earls of Winchilsea and Nottingham. Amongst the records a detailed list of 'fines, forfeitures and amerciaments sett presented and affeered at the Court Leet and Court Baron of Sir Heneage Finch Knt. and Bart' in October 1673 gives a clear idea of what the court was doing at that time.[28] First, it lists the names of 38 butchers, all fined 3s. 4d. 'for not bringing hide and tallow with the flesh to the market' and thus depriving tallow chandlers, curriers and tan-ners of the materials of their trades. Next there is a list of 18 bakers, almost all from out of town, fined the same sum for breaking the Assize of Bread, by giving short weight. Then comes a list

of five poulterers fined 5s. each for 'forestalling the market', selling on market day before trading officially commenced. Next to be fined were 23 householders 'for their dirt in the Streete before their dores', who were all fined the standard 3s. 4d., except two, who were given double fines. Under 'Common trespass and other defaults', 39 people were listed, nearly all of whom were fined for offences under the regulations of the open fields. A few trespasses were concerned with innholders blocking the streets with wagons and timber, and the wellmasters at Jessons well were amerced 'for the Buckett being in the well when the fire began att Richard Glenns'. There was also a list of people who had not paid their levies 'to Jessons Well'. Nineteen were listed as 'de-faulters for not appearing or essoineing' (payments for non-attendance at court), and two men received a swingeing fine of 40 shillings each for refusing to serve after being chosen constable—a reminder that men chosen for manorial or parish office were compelled to serve or else face the consequences. Finally, under the heading 'Bloudshedds', John Pike was fined 3s.4d. 'for committing a bloudshed on the body of William Usher', whilst Jane Seely, John Church and Widow Allibone were fined double that for 'affronting the constables in their office'.

Court rolls for later in the 18th century show that some of the powers of the manorial court were ceasing to be enforced. However, street nuisances are plentifully recorded, including, in addition to those listed above, fines of butchers for killing animals in the streets outside their shops 'to the great annoyance of the inhabitants'. They also contain information about the other manorial of-ficers. The two respectable ratepayers who were nominated to serve as constables had three men to assist them as 'thirdboroughs', paid deputy-con-stables, two for Daventry and one for Drayton. For the working of the open fields, the manorial court each year appointed three pasture masters and three fieldsmen and a hayward for Daventry and for Drayton. Two pumpmasters were appointed for each of the five town pumps, and another wellmaster for St Austin's well, two leather sealers for the inspection of leather on sale, two bread weighers and ale tasters and two flesh tasters to inspect food sold in the markets and fairs. With the exception of those relating to the open fields, all these officers continued to be appointed into the 19th century.

In the second half of the 18th century the manorial court gradually lost some of its main functions. Meeting only once a year and exercising little control over its officers, and lacking the power to levy a rate, it was gradually superseded by new legislation, and saw some of its powers pass to other authorities, such as the vestry, and, after 1805, to the Daventry Street Commissioners. The major blow to the manorial court were the Acts which enclosed the common fields. The first came in 1753, when Drayton was enclosed. In the case of Daventry, the old land system lasted another half century, so there the court continued to fulfil its age-old function for that part of the manor.

The decline of his manor court probably gave Sir Heneage Finch and his successors little cause for worry: court profits were a minor part of the income he derived from his lordship. His manorial rights included the tolls of the markets and the oldest of the fairs, the ownership of the town bakehouse and malt mill, which had the monopolies of baking all the household bread and grinding all the malt produced in the town. He also owned the Moot Hall, which included the Sessions room, gaol and butchers shambles adjoining, and, from the early 18th century, the rents and profits of a waterworks for supplying the town with soft water from a spring on Borough Hill. The value of his properties is revealed in a detailed rental for the year 1669, its contents being itemised under five headings:

in kind as well as cash. These occur in the form of capons, a pound of pepper, two turkeys and, in two cases, a 'hare pye'. 'The Great Rents were mainly for yardlands and closes, though the £40 rent paid by the corporation for the baileywick was included under this heading. John Bardoll, draper, paid £60 for his land, William Clarke £46 for land in Drayton, and John Manley £46 for the Inlands and Rumbelows the two great town closes, £9 for 'Priors Furs' and £36 for a farm in Drayton. He also appears in the 'Small Rents' list, paying £1 13s. 4d. and the above-mentioned hare pie for a piece of 'furs and six leyes', and 5s. and two capons for another piece of furze 'called burnt walls'. The seven 'Guild lands' were the endowments of the long-dissolved medieval guild. The 'Small Rents' and 'Concealed Rents' were for 'little houses', gardens and small parcels of land: they yielded the lord from 3s. 4d. to £2.[29]

Between 1666 and 1786, the year the Finch family sold their Daventry estate, the income doubled, being over £1,000 by the latter year. The purchasers were a consortium consisting of John Plomer Clarke of Welton, and four prominent Daventry figures—Thomas Freeman, attorney, Charles Watkins, draper and banker, William Cullingworth, bookseller and stationer, and Henry Bagshaw Harrison, attorney and town clerk. Together they put up the purchase money of £21,673 and agreed to divide the property between them.[30] Clarke was chief investor. It

	Number	Total Rent		
		£	s.	d.
'Quit Rents'	110	10	12	11
'The Great Rents	19	489	16	8
'For Guild Lands'	7	38	18	8
'Small Rents'	25	21	1	10
'Concealed Rents'	16	4	1	6
Totals	177	£564	11	7

Rents in Daventry and Drayton due to Sir Heneage Finch, 25 March 1669

The small annual quit rents ranged from as high as seven shillings for 'the parke and Abbey land' down to sixpences for humble cottages and gardens. One feature here, and under certain of the other rents, is that some tenants paid the lord

enabled him extend his existing holdings in Drayton and to consolidate his Welton Place estate. He also acquired the manorial rights of Daventry and these remained in the Clarke family down to the 20th century.

The local government of Daventry and Drayton was shared by the parish vestry, an assembly in which the ratepayers had their voice. As an institution, the vestry became more important as the manorial court declined. Through its officers, unpaid and compelled upon pain of fines if they refused to serve, were administered poor relief, paving and lighting and the maintenance of the fabric of the parish church and churchyard. For these tasks the parish officers were, respectively, the overseers of the poor, the surveyors of highways and the churchwardens. Of all the tasks undertaken by the vestry, by far the most onerous and expensive was that of poor relief. In pre-Industrial England the proportion of the poor and potentially poor to the total population was high. In the Hearth Tax List for Daventry in 1674 no less than 45 per cent of the houses were excused payment. As the figures below indicate, expenditure on the poor grew decade by decade, though probably not greater that the growth in the population. However, from the 1770s it started to increase and it accelerated rapidly after the Wars against the French commenced in the 1790s. None of this was peculiar to Daventry. After 1815 the poverty question became a national one and ultimately led to a new system poor relief in 1834.

At a vestry meeting in 1774 consideration was given to building near Gin Lane, on land given by William Rose. A committee was set up to supervise the plan and sell the old poorhouse. However, a minute of 1775 in the Vestry Book refers to repairing the poor house and clearing the ditch that ran by it, so it would appear that this project was abandoned.[32]

Charity always had a role in English poor relief, and between 1576 and 1762 a number of small charities were founded, the earliest of which, as we have seen, was that of William Parker, founder of the Free Grammar School, who also left £10 a year to the maintenance of six beadsmen, or weekly pensioners.[33] This was augmented in 1743 by John Sawbridge, who left the beadsmen the interest on an investment of £100. Until 1863, when a new scheme was introduced by the Charity Commissioners, beadsmen were elected by the Bailiff and burgesses when a vacancy arose. In 1624 Bryan Abbey left £60, the interest of which was to be distributed in loaves to 12 poor people weekly. In 1656 Timothy Newton, 'of Middleburgh in Zealand, merchant, born in Daventry', left the interest of £100 'to be given yearly to the most indigent poor of Daventry'. Between the Restoration and the close of the 18th century there

Decade	Average expenditure on the poor £	Decade	Average expenditure on the poor £
1720s	154	1780s	627
1730s	135	1790s	726
1740s	174	1800s	1023
1750s	239	1810s	1547
1760s	277	1820s	1369
1770s	441		

Average expenditure on the poor in Daventry for certain years in each decade, 1720 to 1830[31]

Traditionally, Daventry tried to exclude people likely to make demands upon the parish. Vagrants and beggars were moved on by the parish constable, and a poor house at Brook End was opened for those too old or feeble to maintain themselves. In attempts to economise on its cost, the vestry farmed out the maintaining of the poor, with mixed results, as elsewhere. On occasions the parish considered building a new model workhouse.

were eight more charitable bequests to the poor, in addition to that of John Sawbridge for the beadsmen already noted. Three were benefactions by women for the benefit of poor widows. The other five were those of Richard Farmer, who, as we have seen, in addition to augmenting the minister's stipend, left a £10 annuity to be distributed twice yearly to the poor; that of Hannah Slough, who, in 1684, left £60, the fruits thereof to be employed at the discretion of the burgesses for the benefit of the poor; that of Erasmus Dryden, who in 1708 left £100, the produce of which was to be distributed yearly; that of John Smart, who left a similar sum to be distributed in bread every Sunday 'to such poor people as come constantly to church'; and that of John Watters who, in 1762, left £210, the income from which was to be given to six 'poor honest men'. And, as already noted, there was the bequest of Edward Sawbridge for the apprenticing of the son of one honest poor person in the parish each year. In the late 17th and early 18th centuries it was also common for small sums of money to be distributed to the poor, some times by the executors of wills and sometimes by the minister.

By the late 18th century the burgesses and trustees of the town charities were responsible for the administration of several estates in which some of the benefactions had been invested, the rents from which formed the principle income of the charities. These consisted of the 73 acres in Upper Boddington, a freehold 'poor's close' in Drayton and part shares with the English Charity School in the estate at Woodford, near Thrapston. The trustees also received payments out of the Christ Church estate and a fixed rent charge payable out of the Parker estate at Upwick Hall, Hertfordshire, for the beadsmen. In addition, the money from a number of the above bequests were invested in Consols. In the early 19th century the finances of the charities became involved in a tangle with those of the Moot Hall, and there was the problem of corporation trusteeship after the corporation had been abolished in 1835. Eventually the matter was sorted out in a scheme devised by the Charity Commissioners in 1863, who appointed a body of nine trustees to administer the municipal charities. Daventry's charities were useful for relieving the 'deserving' poor— widows, aged persons and orphans. Because they were 'recommending' charities, trustees had freedom to choose whom they supported and rejected. They were also biased towards those who attended church, so Daventry Dissenters established their own. And, useful as charities were to the town, their income should not be exaggerated. At the end of the 19th century it amounted to about £150 a year and not all of it was spent on the poor.

Private enterprise had a role in local government. The most notable example in Georgian times was the waterworks. Its early history is told in a tripartite agreement of 1715 between Daniel, Earl of Nottingham, Baron Finch of Daventry, Obediah Smith, bookseller, and Robert Crofts, turner, and John Smith, bookseller. It recites how Crofts and Obediah Smith did 'some years since make and mound a free stone wall … in a certain piece of ground lying and being in a certain place called the New Conduit on the North side of Borough Hill called the Redway, a cistern for holding water'. Into this they laid pipes from the Old Conduit Springs on the hill to the cistern, and from there laid pipes 'down the Redway' to Daventry for the supply of water 'into the houses of such of the inhabitants … as should think fitt to make use of and agree with them for the same'.

The trouble was that Smith and Crofts did so without leave of the Earl, owner of the land on which the cistern and pipes were laid. He caused the pipes to be pulled up and the flow of water to the town ceased. However, by an agreement made in 1706, the two proprietors received a 21-year lease from the Earl and resumed supplies. By 1715 'the said pipes being wood pipes and much decayed', Smith and Crofts, unwilling to face the cost of replacement, agreed to part with their interest to John Smith, who agreed to lay lead pipes from the cistern to the town at his own cost and take over the residue of the lease from the Earl. The enterprising bookseller also made an agreement with the Earl for a further lease of 99 years to commence in 1727, at a rent of 40 shillings per annum. He further agreed to keep water in a pond near the cistern for the watering of cattle and sheep pastured on the town common there. For those who could afford it, the supply of pure soft water to the town was a valuable asset, in a period when most people had to rely on well-water. It was also reasonably profitable to the proprietor. When offered for sale in 1834 the waterworks were said to produce an income of 'upwards of £100 per annum'.[34]

ECONOMIC AND SOCIAL DEVELOPMENTS 1660 TO 1790

Population growth

In the late 17th and early 18th centuries, travellers through Daventry who left impressions of the place agree as to its prosperity. Blome, in 1673, noted it 'hath a *Market* on *Wednesdays* which is well served with *horses, cattle, sheep, corn,* and *provisions*'. Celia Fiennes in the 1690s remembered Daventry as 'a pretty large market town and good houses all of stone'. About 1712, John Morton commented that Daventry 'stands upon the same road with Towcester and is of Note for its Good Inns, and has a flourishing Trade; being reckon'd a Town of very good Business'. And, soon afterwards, Daniel Defoe saw it as a 'considerable market town which subsists chiefly by the great concourse of travellers on the old Watling Street way'.[35] In the period from the Restoration to the early Victorian era, market towns all over England, especially those located on major national routes, enjoyed what for many of them were their greatest years. This was certainly true of Daventry.

As we have seen, the population between 1676 and 1801 almost doubled (from 1,450 to 2,582). Judging by the relationship between burials and baptisms recorded in the parish registers, this growth was anything but steady. Between 1660 and 1709 each decade saw an excess of baptisms over burials. This impression of population expansion is put into reverse in the period 1710 to 1759. In these years each decade saw an excess of burials over baptisms, the 1740s and 1750s being the decades with the greatest number. Then, in line with national trends, from 1760 to the end of the 1790s, there was an excess of baptisms over burials once more, the 1790s (with 120) seeing the largest total for any decade since 1660. These figures are subject to a number of reservations as a base for accurate population statistics, but there is no reason to suspect that they do not reflect in general what was happening.

As we have seen, Daventry largely escaped the plague in 1665, no more than twenty dying of it that year. In the 18th century the terror of the plague was replaced by the terror of smallpox. This disease was probably responsible for the high mortality in 1711, when 89 burials were recorded, against a yearly average of 41 in that decade. The worst visitation was in 1737, when within 12 months 102 deaths were recorded, double the yearly average at that time. Another was in 1754, when 67 were carried off by that disease. The effects of such visitations were not merely personal. They seriously affected the trade of the town. When infection subsided it was necessary to inform people in the *Northampton Mercury* that it was safe to come again.[36] The threat of the smallpox led to attempts at preventive

medicine. In 1755 Mr. Fraunces, a Daventry apothecary, inoculated 500 people at his house in Everdon, and this was a practice long continued. In 1794-5 we hear of Daventry doctors superintending inoculation houses in Charwelton and Floore.[37] Whether this was responsible for the decline in virulence of the disease in the second half of the century is debatable. What is certain is that after 1750 fewer people died of the smallpox. From then the population of this country began to increase and has never stopped.

Inns and wayfaring

A resolution in the Borough Assembly Book in 1754 noted a 'great increase of Publick houses within this Borough'. By the early 19th century there were some 27 licensed houses in the town. How many were inns is not easy to ascertain, especially before the later 18th century, though the *Wheat Sheaf*, the *Saracen's Head*, the *Plough and Bell* and the *Brown Bear*, being the houses from which coaches left Daventry in 1824, certainly were. Others, such as the *Swan*, though in decline by this time, had once been prominent. The principle functions of the inns were to provide means of transport and what the advertisements of the time called 'every convenient office for the accommodation of travellers'. Although there had been a regular coach service between Birmingham and London since 1731, down to the later 18th century most travellers either went on foot or by horseback. Before the era of regular and frequent coaches, posting or horse-hiring was a primary function of the inns. Two mid-18th-century advertisements to let the *Saracen's Head* illustrate this. They stated it had stabling for 50 horses, that it was 'commodiously situated on the great Post Road from London to Chester' and that there was 'employment for three Chaises and ten Horses in the Posting-Business'.[38] It has been pointed out that the Stuart inn was not only a hotel but a warehouse, a bank, an exchange, an auction room, a scrivener's office and a coach and wagon park. By 1700 it had also become a posting house and an information bureau for the commercial facilities of the area. By 1800 it was involved in a fast-developing system of Royal Mails and long-distance coaching. It was also by then providing suitable accommodation for much of the respectable entertainment in the town.

NOTICE is hereby given, That a Meeting of the Trustees,
appointed by Act of Parliament for repairing the Highways from Old-Stratford, in the County of Northampton, to the
Dun Cow, in Dunchurch, in the County of Warwick, will be
held by Adjournment, at the WHEAT SHEAF INN, in DAVENTRY,
on TUESDAY, the 5th Day of MAY next, at Eleven o'Clock in
the Forenoon, at which Meeting the TOLLS to arise for one
Year at the Toll-Gates hereunder mentioned, will be LETT to
FARM to the Best Bidder, in Manner directed by the Statute
made in the 13th Year of his Majesty's Reign, for regulating
Turnpike-Roads, which Tolls produced in the last Year, over
and above the Charges for collecting the same, the several Sums
following, that is to say,

    The Gate at Old-Stratford £588
    The Gate at Stow-Hill 590
    The Gate at Drayton-Lane 595

And will be severally put up at such Sums as the Trustees shall
direct. Whoever happens to be the Best Bidders must forthwith
pay £50 in Advance for each Gate, and produce sufficient
Sureties, and give Security for Payment of the Residue of the
Rents, at such Times and Manner as the Trustees shall direct.

    And Notice is hereby further given, That the Trustees will at
the same Meeting, take into Consideration, and determine upon
the Propriety of erecting a Ticket-Gate, or other Turnpike-Gate,
or Bar across the Turnpike-Road at Stow-Hill, South of Hey-
ford-Lane; and also erecting another Ticket-Gate, or other Turnpike-Gate or Bar, across the said Road, at some proper Place
between Foster's Booth and Towcester.—Dated the 2d Day of
April, 1812.   EDMUND BURTON,
                                                  Clerk to the said Trustees.

36   Notice in the *Northampton Mercury*, 1812, regarding the letting of the tolls on the turnpike road through Daventry.

Landlords of the major inns were often rich and important figures. Many came from out of town and retired elsewhere in old age. We find evidence of them in their wills and in newspaper advertisements. In his will of 1695, Jonathan Matthew, owner of the *Wheat Sheaf*, left no less than £1,300 in cash to his seven children, a greater sum than in any other Daventry will of the period.[39] However, before taking over he had been a successful Daventry mercer and draper, serving as Bailiff in 1673-4 and 1683-4. Some,

such as William Smith, came into the business from service. When he took the *Swan* in 1797, he announced himself as 'late butler to John Clarke Esq., Welton Place'. The same year, John Grimshaw, taking the *Dun Cow*, came from Warwick, where he had been a horse dealer. In 1781 Sarah Brooke announced that she was retiring from the *Wheat Sheaf* in favour of her son-in-law, John Ashworth, who, holding the tenancy on a building lease, was soon improving the lodging rooms by enclosing the gallery round the court yard. The ambitious Mr. Ashworth did not live long enough to see his plans come to fruition, for within a short time we find his widow announcing that she intended to carry on the business.[40]

With the growth of inland trade there developed a pressing need to improve the state of the roads. At a time when their upkeep was regarded as a local rather than a national responsibility, the device chosen was the characteristic one of the local Act of Parliament. This gave legal sanction to a Turnpike Trust, empowered to take over the management of a particular stretch of road. Costs would be recouped though tolls collected at turnpike gates, and the first call on profits would be to pay the income on capital invested in the Trust. The first roads to be turnpiked were national routes, the first through Northamptonshire being the stretch of the Chester road from Old Stratford to Dunchurch, passing though Daventry, the first Act for which was passed in 1707. Some time was to elapse before the other, cross-country, routes through the town came under this system. The Warwick to Northampton and Banbury to Lutterworth roads had to wait until 1765. Turnpike trusts became important local institutions: the gentry, professions and tradesmen invested in them, as did widows seeking annuities. Solicitors handled their business, contractors repaired them, innkeepers hosted their quarterly meetings, newspapers printed their announcements. The trusts undoubtedly improved the main roads. What they did not do, however, was to provide top quality roads. There was a time-lag between their formation and the introduction of improved methods of road construction, which came in towards the end of the century. Nor did they please road users, for whom the turnpike gates were an irritant to be avoided where possible and suffered when avoidance was inevitable.

The users of the great road and the inns also remain shadowy, though occasional incidents give some insight into early 18th-century traffic. In 1736, for instance, the driver of a wagon belonging to one Woods of Liverpool, 'a common carrier between that place and the City of London' was taken before Bailiff Edward Sawbridge, for driving a large wagon drawn by seven horses 'in length contrary to the statute in that case made and provided, which said wagon was not employed in Husbandry but loaded with Goods'.[41] The Act

was intended to prevent wagons so large that their weight damaged the surface of the road. One category of traveller who does appear with some frequency in local records is the soldier. Daventry, like other road towns, was the scene of many a quartermaster's activities. In late 1694 the minister baptised children of Dutch troopers in the army of William III, returning, perhaps, from the defeat of James II in Ireland. Earlier in that year he buried Theophilus Gardner, 'an Ensigne in Collonel Brudenel's Regiment, killed this day by his Lieutenant in a Rancounter in the Sheaf-yard'. In 1740 the rough soldiery appear in a somewhat more humane light when the churchwardens distributed one hundred sixpenny loaves amongst the poor, the money having been collected 'by the Gentlemen in Major Nazoon's Troop, in her late Majesty's Regiment … now lying at Daventry'.[42]

Where navigable rivers were absent, as they were in the Daventry area, country produce moved to the London market by carrier's wagon. Apart from one mention in the register of freemen in 1677, the earliest reference to a Daventry carrier in this period dates from 1754.[43] In that year John Adams was advertising his twice weekly service for goods and passengers to and from London. Bailiff in 1749-50, Adams died in 1758, but his business survived and for many years it

ANN ADAMS, Daventry *Carrier.*
TAKES this Opportunity of returning Thanks to all her kind Customers, and to assure 'em, that the utmost Care shall be taken of all Goods that are sent by her; but as Mistakes have happened, for want of proper Directions, she desires all Gentlemen and Tradesmen for the future will please to order their Correspondents in London to direct their Goods *To go by* ADAMS *from the Rose-and-Crown in St. John's Street,* for want of which it often happens that Porters carry them to wrong Inns, and they are sent by other Carriers, by which means Gentlemen are disappointed, and she, without Cause, gets Anger.——She continues as usual to set out from London every Monday and Thursday Morning at Eight o'Clock, and returns to Daventry every Wednesday and Saturday; and carries Goods and Passengers to Stony-Stratford, Towcester, Daventry, Rugby, and all Places adjacent, at the most reasonable Rates: And as the Waggons go and return from London in so short a Time, they are as convenient as Coaches, or any other Carriages, for Hares, Venison, Fish, &c. Constant Attendance is given at the Rose-and-Crown aforesaid, and at her House in Daventry; and those who please to employ her, may depend on the greatest Care and Diligence to merit a Continuance of the Favours conferr'd on
Their most humble Servant,
ANN ADAMS.
N. B. She will not be accountable for Cash, Plate, Writings, &c. unless enter'd, and paid for as such.

37 Notice inserted in the *Northampton Mercury* by Ann Adams, the Daventry carrier, 18 February 1760.

had a virtual monopoly of carrying to and from the capital. In 1760 Ann Adams, presumably his widow, was advertising the same route twice weekly to the *Rose & Crown* in St John's Street in the City of London. She was still in business in 1767, at which time the journey to London was taking two days, and the return about thirty-two hours. Mrs. Adams was succeeded by a John Adams, presumably her son. The only other long-distance carrier at this time was John Wodhams, proprietor of the Daventry Stage Wagon: in 1767 he was operating a once-weekly service from the *Swan* to London. By 1791, John Adams' son, William, was the sole London carrier, though there was another—Thomas Adams, perhaps a relative—whose route was from his house in Daventry to the *Dolphin*, Northampton, returning to Daventry and then proceeding to the *White Hart*, Digbeth, Birmingham and thence back to Daventry. In 1807, John Adams carried on the business, having purchased the market wagons, horses and stock-in-trade of his brother, William, upon the latter's death. He did not stay in it long, announcing his retirement three years later, and with him ended the long domination of the trade by the Adams family, which in all had lasted some sixty years.[44] They were succeeded by Amos Packwood, who informed 'Dairymen, Butchers and others, customers to the late Wagons' that he would run two fly-wagons a week to London, getting there in 40 hours. Fourteen years later he was still in business, carrying between London and Holyhead 'up and down every day'. By then there were six other Daventry carriers, two to London, one to Birmingham and three to Northampton.[45]

Daventry's markets and fairs

From 1660 Daventry prospered even more than in the past from the trade brought through its Wednesday market and annual fairs. By 1752 there were five of the latter, and in that year their dates were altered as a result of the 'altera-

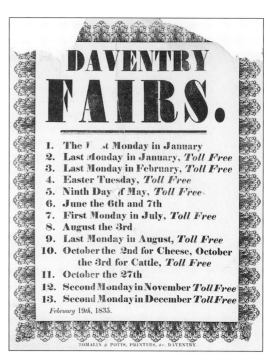

38   Handbill, Daventry Fair dates, 1835.

tion of the style' from the old to the new calendar.

From about 1720 the improvement of local farming led to an emphasis on sheep and stock farming at the expense of the traditional corn and sheep husbandry. In 1760 it was remarked that 'for several years past there have been large quantities of horses, cows, sheep and other cattle sold' at the Beast Fair in August. Such was the amount of business coming into the town that by 1835 the number of Daventry's fairs had grown to thirteen. By then there was also dairying in the district which produced a local cheese: Daventry cheese is said to have been 'a white, small, round, very blue English cheese, similar to Stilton'.[46]

In addition to fairs for beasts and other agricultural produce, there were the statute fairs

Before 1752	1752 and after
Easter Tuesday (and the two following days)	Easter Tuesday
St Augustine's Day cattle fair (26 May)	6 June
Beast Fair two days before St James (23 July)	3 August
Michaelmas fair for cheese, hops, etc. (21-23 Sept)	2 October
'Ram Fair' (16 October)	17 October

Daventry Fairs 1576 to 1752

☞ NOTICE ☜

FAIRS

WILL BE HELD AT

DAVENTRY,

FOR THE SALE OF

CATTLE CHEESE & ONIONS

On Monday, October 3rd, 1887,

AND FOR THE SALE OF

CATTLE

On THURSDAY, October 27th.

THE THREE

MOPS

For HIRING SERVANTS,

WILL BE HELD AT DAVENTRY, ON

WEDNESDAY, OCTOBER 12th, 1887,

AND THE TWO FOLLOWING WEDNESDAYS.

WILLIAM WILLOUGHBY, Mayor.

HAWKSWORTH, PRINTER, DAVENTRY.

39   Handbill, October Fairs, 1887.

AN

A   C   T

FOR

Dividing and Inclofing the Open and Common Fields, Common Paftures, Common Meadows, and other Commonable Lands and Grounds, within the Manor, Parifh, and Liberties of *Daventry*, in the County of *Northampton*.

W̶H̶E̶R̶E̶A̶S̶ the Open and Common Fields, Common Paftures, Common Meadows, and other Commonable Lands and Grounds, lying and being within the Parifh and Liberties of *Daventry*, in the County of *Northampton*, are reputed to contain One Thoufand Six Hundred Acres, or thereabouts:

And whereas *John Clarke*, Efquire, is Lord of the Manor of *Daventry* aforefaid:

And whereas the Dean and Chapter of the Cathedral Church of *Chrift* in *Oxford*, of the Foundation of King *Henry* the Eighth, are feifed of the Rectory and Vicarage Impropriate of the faid Parifh of *Daventry*, and in Right thereof are entitled to all Tythes, both Great and Small, annually arifing, renewing, and increafing within the Parifh and Liberties of *Daventry* (except within the Hamlet of *Drayton*, in the Parifh of *Daventry* aforefaid, and except a certain Piece of Ground called *Common Leys*); and the faid Dean

40   The firft page of the Daventry Enclofure Act, 1802.

at Michaelmas on three successive Wednesdays 'for masters to hire servants and servants to get masters'. The different occupations held their statute at specific public houses; millers, for instance, around 1760, gathering at the *Plume of Feathers*. These hiring fairs and 'mops' were the great annual holiday for farm and domestic servants. Young men and women came into Daventry to enjoy themselves at the sideshows and public houses and to find themselves a master or mistress for the coming year. In Georgian England the boisterous and beery nature of mops and 'stattis' were accepted as part of rural life. The more puritanical Victorian middle classes professed themselves shocked at such scenes and tried to have them suppressed. As the last vestiges of hiring fairs in Daventry did not finally die away until the 1950s, that campaign was clearly not one of their great successes. The statute fair was also the time when parish constables came to Daventry to pay their parish contributions towards the county rate to the chief constable of the hundred.

The end of the open fields

In 1753 the end of 800 years of agricultural history came with the enclosure of the open fields of Drayton. Twenty or thirty years previously those advancing arguments in favour of agricultural improvement began to prevail over those who clung to the traditional organisation system of farming. The chosen instrument of the drive towards total enclosure of the landscape was, once again, the private Act of Parliament. The owners of two thirds of the land in any parish or township with its own field system had to be in agreement to enclose, or else the Bill would not pass in Parliament. Within a century, Northamptonshire, a county where common field farming survived longest, was progressively enclosed, common rights abolished and the scattered holdings of the proprietors consolidated, so that the modern farm could have a 'ring-fence' nature. Instead of farming 'in common', farming was now to be individually.

Before enclosure the farmers of Daventry who were farmers and nothing else went about their business and played no great part in the public life of the town, and only a small proportion of the people of Daventry were agricultural labourers. Yet, being the market town of a rich agricultural district, much of its business was country business. Moreover, townsmen often combined trade with some possession of land or common rights. For instance, the probate inventory of John

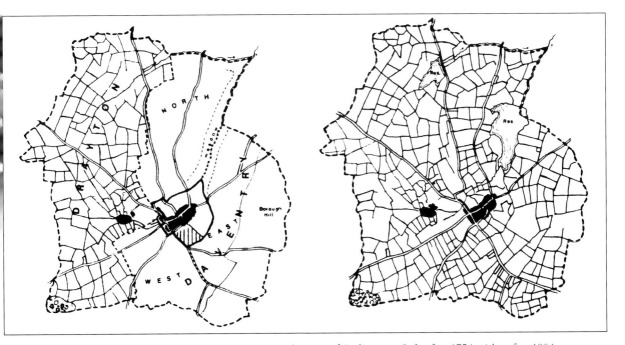

41 The replanning of the fields after enclosure by Act of Parliament. *Left*, after 1754, *right*, after 1804.

Bardoll, draper, dated 1666, values hay and faggots in the 'barn at home', wheat, peas and straw in the abbey barn, three cows, a calf and a yearling at Rumbelows Close, hay, a horse and a malt mill at the Mill House, and a boar and a sow in the Mill Yard in addition to his shop and his household effects.[47] Other 17th-century wills and inventories confirm a pattern of combining a trade with the keeping of animals, a close or two of grassland, and the occasional lease of a yardland of arable land in the open fields. It was natural for them to do so, for, before enclosure, attached to many houses were ancient common rights, which usually meant the right to pasture three horses, three cows and 60 sheep on Borough Hill, and in the arable fields after harvest. These valuable rights of common were always mentioned when premises were advertised for sale.

Drayton was enclosed half a century before Daventry because there were fewer interests to reconcile in order to secure the agreement necessary to satisfy Parliament. After enclosure, just over a third of its 1,500 acres was owned by the Earl of Winchilsea, and, apart from 14 minor proprietors, the rest by the dean and chapter of Christ Church, Oxford (225 acres), John Clarke of Welton (115 acres) and John Watters, who had 140 acres.[48] All these now had their land in reasonably contiguous blocks, the better to let it to tenant farmers. No one was more delighted with his allotment than James Affleck, perpetual curate of Daventry, who was compensated for the loss of his tithe rights by an estate of 50 acres, which brought him considerably more than his lost tithes. The enclosure of Drayton was a major step in the improvement of the living. So was the enclosure of Daventry, which took place half a century later.

At its enclosure in 1802-4, the 1660 acres of the township of Daventry were allocated amongst 60 people, just over two thirds of whom received parcels of less than 10 acres. The greatest beneficiary were the dean and chapter of Christ Church,

allotted (in round figures) 670 acres for the extinguishing of their great tithes, their 15 yardlands and their common rights. Of this, they made 129 acres available to the perpetual curate of Daventry, thus giving his income another substantial boost and freeing him (and themselves) of the tiresome business of tithe forever. The other major landowner was John Clarke, Esq., lord of the manor, whose consolidated estate was 303 acres.[49]

In this major act of re-planning, the greatest since medieval times, the people left out in the process of enclosure were those who inhabited cottages which carried no ancient common rights. Before enclosure, sanctioned by custom and the notion that the poor needed a few resources to survive, they had access to scraps of marginal land. But, as the main object of enclosure was to bring all land into private ownership and under cultivation, their claims to consideration went unrecognised in the enclosure process. After enclosure it was no longer possible for the labourer to practise the 'cottage economy' of his forefathers and it bred a sense of injustice. The only resource he now had was his own labour. Moreover, in a landscape hedged, ditched and gated, access to the fields and the town common on Borough Hill was lost, though some public rights of way survived. Enclosure was a step by which town and country, and property and the propertyless, became more sharply separated.

Trades and occupations

The pattern of the town's economy did not change significantly in this period. It remained one of exchange and small-scale production, providing goods and services for the town, its market area and for wayfarers on the roads. The control of it remained in the hands of the corporation and its freemen's registers provide the basic source of information. Details of freemen registered down to 1835, when the system was replaced by one of free entry into the market, are summarised below:

	Category	1670-1729	1730-1789	1790-1835
1.	Crafts	71	106	128
2.	Retail	33	56	98
3.	Processing trades	27	19	20
4.	Unspecified	2	6	11
	Total freemen	133	187	267

Freemen enrolled in Daventry, 1670 to 1835

Comparing these three periods, the overall numbers of freemen, reflecting general town growth, increased steadily so that in the early 19th century there were twice as many enrolled as a century before. Half were craftsmen. With the exception of the period 1730-89, the craft which enrolled the most (74) was shoemaking. Even so, the cordwainers were not engaged in wholesale production, but were serving the local market for footware. The second most numerous class of craftsmen were those working in wood—carpenters, joiners, turners, coopers and wheelwrights. After them, those making clothing; in the period from 1790 the greatest rise in that category was in tailors. Fourth among the craftsmen came metal workers, there being a significant rise in the numbers of smiths and farriers from 1730 with the increase of road traffic. After them came men involved in the building trades, though it would seem that at any one time there was work for only one master mason or bricklayer, and only one plumber and glazier in Daventry, the sum total over the whole period being only twenty-five.

Two other categories of master craftsmen remain—'fine craftsmen' and leather workers. In these years the former numbered only 15; one painter, one artist and 13 watchmakers. Like many other small towns Daventry turned out timepieces for farmers and the well-to-do. Over this period there were only some 24 master craftsmen working leather, as horse-collar makers, saddlers and whip makers. In the late 18th and 19th centuries Daventry had a reputation for the manufacture of whips. Yet the freemen's registers reveal that no master whipmakers were enrolled before 1729, only one between 1730 and 1789 and seven between then and 1835. The trade was founded by a saddler called John Rose. His firm (by then William Rose & Co.) was the only one making them in any quantity in 1784. Soon after, however, the firm of Barrett & Palmer was formed, becoming Barrett, Palmer & Co. by 1789. Four years later it was Marfell, Jones & Palmer.[50] By then William Rose & Co. were no longer in business. In 1800 there was also the firm of John Dickins, which called itself 'The Original Whip Manufactory' and might have been successor to Rose. Dickins carried on until his death in 1840, when the firm became Thomas Dickins & Co. Just how many workers were employed in this trade is not known, but Daventry's reputation in

whipmaking probably originated in a report of the Board of Agriculture in 1809 which said there was a considerable manufactory of whips in the town 'in which two master-manufacturers each employ an outrider and a number of workmen'.[51]

Over the three periods there was a marked growth in overall numbers of retailers. The numbers of bakers remained remarkably constant. In the case of butchers, fishmongers, greengrocers, confectioners and tea dealers we find no admissions before 1790. Foreigners who came in on market day were prominent in these trades, and before 1790 there was no obligation on Daventry-based shopkeepers to take up their freedoms. This changed from 1790. With grocers another pattern is discernible. In the years 1670 to 1729 only two became freemen; in 1730 to 1789 fourteen; whilst from 1790 the figure was twenty-two. This indication of the increase of retailing in the later 18th century is also shown by the figures for drapers and haberdashers taking up their freedoms.

That Daventry was not a town where any trade was expanded enough to begin to produce on an 'industrial' scale before 1790 is underlined by the tiny scale of textiles and leather-tanning in our period. In the late 17th and early 18th centuries there had been some textile production. Between 1670 and 1729 four weavers, four dyers and two fullers were made free, but the trade faded thereafter. In the rest of the century only one weaver, one woolcomber, one hosier and two framework knitters appear. Spinning and weaving revived in some villages in the district in the second half of the century, Daventry being the market where the jersey yarn and pieces of cloth were sold. In 1763, James England, a Spitalfields master, tried unsuccessfully to establish the trade in the town, but he found better fortune in Weedon Bec, where he gained the reputation of an 'inhuman taskmaster' to the pauper children he employed.[52] Similarly the production of leather, the other processing trade, was on a tiny scale. There was a tanyard in Drayton, but over the course of these 150 years, only 27 men took up their freedoms as curriers, fellmongers, leather dressers, tanners or whittawers.

Registers of freemen do not tell us about the numbers of workers employed by freemen, though all apprentices had to be registered. But because Daventry was a town of small workshops it would not be expected that information on this subject would reveal any different patterns from the ones shown for freemen. An examination of one useful source—the Militia List for 1777—confirms this assumption. This records the names and occupations of men between the ages of 18 and 45, liable to be balloted for militia service. Though there are omissions—poor men with three or more children were exempted—it gives a good idea of the occupational pattern of Daventry. Just over a third were craftsmen, 18 per cent were general labourers, and 12 per cent servants. The fourth largest group were retail workers, and the rest agricultural labourers, people involved in processing, ostlers and other inn servants, and servants working for professional men.[53] For this period little is known about the pay and industrial relations, though one notice in the *Northampton Mercury* in 1752 reveals how wages in one trade were fixed. It states:

> Whereas the Taylors in several Counties and Places have lately raised their wages; this is to give Notice to Master Taylors that live within twelve Miles of Daventry, that they are desired to meet at the Saracen's Head in Daventry, on Wednesday the 11th of this Instant March, at Ten o'clock in the Forenoon, in order to raise and settle the wages of the said business.[54]

As already noted above, professional men were becoming more numerous as the 18th century wore on, and the part played on the corporation by the Wildgooses, a family of surgeons, has been outlined. There were other medical men. In 1751 John Adams, surgeon and apothecary, announced, on entering practice, that 'he hath been fully instructed in every branch of Midwifery by the eminent Dr. Smellie in London, and that he was ready to attend people in need of his services', adding, 'The Poor in Distress, at a moderate Distance, he'll attend gratis'.[55] By 1784 there were four firms of attorneys, and the bank of Charles Watkins and John Smith, both originally drapers, had come into existence. Traditionally, Daventry's richest burgesses came from that particular trade, so it is perhaps no surprise that, with the rise of country banks, Daventry's first one should have been started by two drapers. By 1791 there was also Riley & Shaw, Bankers, Drapers and Agents for the Sun Fire Office.[56]

By that decade the economy of Daventry was on the verge of change in other ways. The manufacturing of boots and shoes was about to commence, and this coincided with the further growth of Daventry as a market centre. There was also the stimulus brought by the development of the Holyhead Road, the M1 of its day, which ushered in 'the golden age of coaching'.

Sport and pleasure in Georgian Daventry

Daventry not only drew in people from the country around for business and shopping but also began to organise sporting and other entertainments for them. The first of these, from which some of the others seem to have sprung, were the races. There is mention of them as early as 1696 and they were held annually, with certain gaps, from 1724 to 1742. The course was a circuit within the ancient earthworks on the top of Borough Hill. In the 1720s and early '30s the races were a three-day summer meeting between June and September. In 1733 there were no races. It is not clear why: there may have been an epidemic or cattle sickness but it may have been because of competition from one of the other race meetings in the area. Possibly local interest was flagging, because from 1730 prize-money started to fall, and the subscriptions of innholders to the Town Plate had to be doubled to 10 shillings. The races restarted the following year, though prize money was still reduced, and in 1735 the meeting became a two-day one. It was therefore decided to make the races more of a social occasion with the introduction of a Ball at the *Wheat Sheaf*. For three years from 1736 the races were again interrupted, this time because of the smallpox. When they recommenced in 1739 they were moved to Whit week, and an attempt was made to lay on extra entertainment. The public were informed that there would be Cocking each morning, with a Ball for the entertainment of the ladies each night. It was a pattern which lasted only a few years. Horse racing on a regular basis in Daventry ended in 1742.[57]

Cock fighting, however, continued. For some years after its inception, the cockpit at the *Wheat Sheaf* saw annual mains of 21 cocks a side with so much per battle for the owners, plus a prize for winning the whole main. For spectators there was the double excitement of the fights and betting. Here, as at the races, the 'Quality' rubbed shoulders with the common people. Sometimes cocks were put up by syndicates, such as 'the Gentlemen of Northamptonshire', whose invariable opponents were 'the Gentlemen of

DAVENTRY RACES.

ON Tuefday in Whitfon Week next will be run for on Borough-Hill, near Daventry, in the County of Northampton, a Purfe of Thirty Guineas, by Hunters not under fix Years old, that have never ftarted for any Plate or Prize, carrying twelve Stone, the beft of three Heats, four Miles to a Heat, paying two Guineas Entrance, or four Guineas at the Poft, the Stakes to go to the fecond-beft Horfe, &c. and five Shillings to be paid to the Clerk of the Race for entring each Horfe, &c.

On Wednefday in Whitfon Week will be run on the fame Courfe a Purfe of Twenty Guineas, by Galloways carrying nine Stone each, all under to be allowed Weight for Inches, the beft of three Heats, four Miles to a Heat, to pay one Guinea Entrance, or three Guineas at the Poft, and five Shillings to the Clerk of the Race.

And on Thurfday in Whitfon Week will be run for on the fame Courfe, a Purfe of Forty Guineas, by any Horfe, Mare or Gelding that never ftarted for any Plate or Prize, each Horfe, &c. to carry twelve Stone, the beft of three Heats, four Miles to a Heat; each Contributor to pay one Guinea Entrance, and a Non-Contributor to pay three Guineas Entrance, or Double Entrance at the Poft, to the Clerk of the Race, the Stakes to go to the fecond-beft Horfe, and five Shillings to be paid to the Clerk of the Race for the Entrance of each Horfe, &c.

All the Horfes, Mares or Geldings that fhall run for the above Prizes, to be fhewed and entred at the Wheat-Sheaff in Daventry on Thurfday the 7th Day of June next, and to ftand at fuch Houfes only as fubfcribe Half a Guinea towards the Town Plate, from the Time of Entrance to the Time of Running.

N. B. There will be a Cock Match between two neighbouring Gentlemen each of the faid Days at the Wheat Sheaff aforefaid; and a Ball at Night.

42   Notice of Daventry Races in the *Northampton Mercury*, 14 May 1739.

> **A** Maine of COCKS will be fought at the Wheat-Sheaff in Daventry on Friday the 25th Inftant, to fhew 21 Cocks a Side, for four Guineas a Battle, and ten Guineas the Maine. There will be an Ordinary at the faid Houfe.

43 Notice of cock-fighting in the *Northampton Mercury*, 14 March 1743.

Warwickshire'. Sometimes local squires did battle on an individual basis, as in 1748, when Valentine Knightley of Fawsley challenged Edward Clarke of Watford. After 1749 the sport was held on a more irregular basis, but as late as 1780 a battle was advertised to take place at the *Black Horse* between the Gentlemen of Northamptonshire and Warwickshire 'to shew 31 cocks on each side, 21 mains and 10 byes: To fight in Siver Heels, for four Guineas a Battle and 40 Guineas the Main', and the two counties put cocks into the same pit again in 1782.[58] But from this time on, largely because of the growing influence of the Evangelical Revival, cock-fighting, together with other of the grosser and more brutal sports of the 18th century, came under increasing moral disapproval. This did not stop them going on, but they became more hole-in-the-corner and no longer advertised in the public prints.

The more genteel pastimes of balls and Assemblies long outlasted the races which first popularised them. As we have seen, balls were introduced in 1739, and became the highlight of the social life of the upper ranks of society. The introduction of the Assembly, that characteristic feature of polite society in the 18th century, was made in 1762 by the enterprising Mrs. Adams, the Daventry carrier on 17 June at the *Wheat Sheaf* and there were four others in the following three months.[59] Very soon Assemblies were beginning and ending with a ball, and became a feature of the winter, rather than the summer, season. From the 1770s to as late as the 1850s it was the custom to have four Assemblies between late October and March. The venue was usually the *Wheat Sheaf*, though other inns, such as the *Saracen's Head*, also built Assembly Rooms. By the 1840s an elaborate hierarchy of polite mid-winter entertainments had emerged. In January 1847, for instance, there was a 'County Ball' at the *Wheat Sheaf*, the somewhat less expensive

annual Card and Dancing Assembly at the *Plough and Bell*, and the annual 'Tradesman's Ball' at the *Saracen's Head*, less expensive than the *Plough and Bell* event.[60]

When Mrs. Adams introduced Assemblies she was capitalising on the dancing craze of the time. Advertisements appeared offering to teach both adults and children, and dancing masters came to Daventry to give demonstrations of the latest dances. Balls were held whenever an excuse presented itself. The recovery of George III from a bout of insanity in 1789 was one. Others were held for the Ladies Boarding School, no doubt as a way of introducing the girls into polite society. Concerts, often combined with balls, also became popular. On 8 December 1777 there was a morning concert in the church of 'the most admired pieces' from Handel's 'Messiah', followed in the evening by a concert of vocal and instrumental music in the *Wheat Sheaf* Assembly Room, followed by a ball.[61]

Another popular pastime was theatre-going. In the second half of the century travelling companies of players found it worth their while to stop in Daventry on their way from spas such as Cheltenham to Northampton and Leicester. One of the earliest to advertise was Messrs. Kennedy and Booth's Company of Comedians, who, at Easter 1770, played *Othello* and a farce *The King and Miller of Mansfield*, and were prevailed on 'by Desire of Mrs. Scriven's Boarding School' to prolong their stay and perform *The Provok'd Husband*.[62] Before 1799 performances were in temporary premises, but in that year a little theatre was opened. It was launched by 'Their Majesties Servants' the company of Messrs Watson and Richards, from the Theatre Royal, Cheltenham, who had arrived in February. For four weeks they gave performances ranging from the classics to melodrama and love stories, and followed that season with five weeks of benefit performances. This theatre established regular theatrical

44   The Georgian Assembly Rooms at the *Saracen's Head* (L.G. Tooby).

Circus Royal,

SARACEN'S HEAD INN YARD,
DAVENTRY.

BOXES 1s. PIT 6d. GALLERY 3d.
Grand Balloon Asscension at 7 o'Clock.

On SATURDAY, September 6 1845,
FOR THE BENEFIT OF

MR. H. BROWN,
CLOWN TO HER MAJESTY,
—ooosubjectsooo—

PROGRAMME OF NEW AND BRILLIANT ENTERTAINMENTS.

MONS. MAUS,
In his extraordinary Performance as the

AIR WALKER.

HERR LUDOVIC LONDELLE,
In his unrivalled

JUGGLING ACT.

MRS. HICKIN'S GRACEFUL EVOLUTIONS ON THE

TIGHT ROPE,
This Act will be enlivened by the WHIMSICALITIES of the

CLOWNS,
Messrs. BULLOCK & BROWN, introducing the MOCK FIGHT AND DYING SCENE.—A DUET ON

TWO HALFPENNY TRUMPETS !

MR. HICKIN,
The First British Horseman, as

SHAW, THE LIFE GUARDSMAN!

MASTER HENRY,
As the Youth of Olymphus.

MR. HICKIN & MR. HANLON
In their Classical Delineations of

GRECIAN AND VENETIAN STATUES;
To be followed by

MR. H. BROWN,
As the GO-A-HEAD DARKEY, who will on a raised Pedestal, give his celebrated

Nigger Statues !

Concluding with the song of the "BOATMAN DANCE" and "JIM ALONG JOSEY, in which he will show " de science ob de Heel and de caperbilities ob de Stampadoes in de Grape Vine Twist, de Cow Chalker, and de Squash Holler Hornpipe.

45 Handbill of the visit of the Circus Royal to the *Saracen's Head* Yard, 1845.

performances by visiting players, which continued despite the burning down of the original theatre in 1803. Seven years later the New Theatre was opened with a performance of *Macbeth*. In 1838 it was replaced by a more modern theatre, 'completely fitted up and lighted with gas'.[63]

Of the more plebeian pastimes, other than the riot over football in 1676 and the betting on horse-racing and cock-fighting, we know little. We have no record of bear, bull or badger-baiting, though they were common elsewhere. In a market town well supplied with public houses we may assume that the common people took their pleasure there. And, each year, in an apparently endless cycle, there was all the fun of the fair.

Seven

Zenith of a Road Town: Daventry 1790 to 1840

The golden age of coaching

In the late 1780s the pattern of coaching was changed by the introduction of mail coaches. Before that time the royal mails were carried on horseback by post-boys or mailmen. In 1782 John Palmer put forward a plan for the mails to be carried by coach. Maintaining strict timetables, the mails were to be run by stage-coach proprietors under licence from the government, at a fixed cost of three pence per mile (the same cost as by post-boy). The additional costs and the profits of the proprietors would be met by carrying parcels and passengers. Horses and coaches would be provided by the contractor, but the guards would be the employees of the Post Office. Palmer's plan was adopted. Although stage coaches soon responded to the challenge, the mails, keeping to strict schedules and running through the night, were for a long time markedly more efficient. Uniformly and handsomely decorated in black and maroon, their coachmen and guards (the latter in their top hats and frogged scarlet coats) were imposing figures and they soon acquired great prestige and public acclaim. This rubbed off on the inns where they stopped: in Daventry these were the *Wheat Sheaf* and the *Plough and Bell*. The mail was not only the fastest means of transport, it was also the fastest means of communication: it carried the news of the day. By the 1830s British mail coaches represented the most efficient system of land transport in the world.[1]

The early triumph of the royal mails was made possible by improvements in coach design and in road making, the latter chiefly associated with the work of two great civil engineers of the time, Telford and Macadam. One of Telford's greatest projects was the making of the Holyhead Road. This was a result of the Union between Great Britain and Ireland in 1801. With the transfer of Irish Members of Parliament to

Westminster there was a need to improve communications between London and Dublin. The shortest crossing to the Emerald Isle was Holyhead-Howth, but the road both east and west of Shrewsbury was poor. With a view to improvement, the government asked Telford to survey the roads to Holyhead. Work began in 1816 and the huge project was not finally completed until the 1830s, but, even before the Menai Bridge was opened in 1826, mail coaches were running through to Holyhead. Telford's task

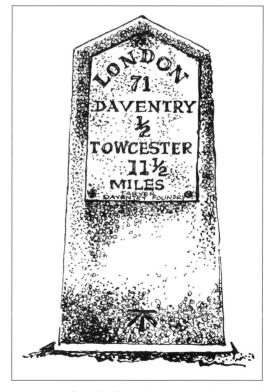

46 One of Telford's mileposts, London Road, Daventry. The iron plate was cast by Tarver, Foundry Place, High Street (L.G. Tooby).

69

Time	Coach	From	To	Inn called at	Days
	NIGHT (am.)				
1.30am	Express	London	Liverpool		daily
2.00am	Standard	London	Liverpool		Not Sunday
2.00am	Reliance	Birmingham	London		W., F., Sat
2.30am	Standard	Liverpool	London	*Plough & Bell*	daily
3.00am	Albion	London	Birmingham	*Plough & Bell*	daily
4.00am	Greyhound	London	Birmingham	*Dun Cow*	daily
4.00am	Royal Mail	London	Liverpool	*Plough & Bell*	daily
4.00am	Royal Mail	London	Holyhead	*Plough & Bell*	daily
4.30am	Emerald	London	Birmingham		daily
5.30am	Reliance	London	Birmingham		T., Th., Sat
	MORNING (am.)				
8.30am	Accommodation	Rugby	London	*Brown Bear*	M., W., Th
10.11	Eclipse Tally-ho	Birmingham	London		daily
10.15	Express	Liverpool	London		daily
10.45	Tally-ho	Birmingham	London	*Saracen's Head*	daily
11.00	Independent	Birmingham	London		daily
11.00	Rising Sun	Cambridge	London	*Wheat Sheaf*	M., W., F., Sat
11.30	Crown Prince	Birmingham	London		daily
	AFTERNOON (pm.)				
1.00pm	Royal Mail	Liverpool	London	*Wheat Sheaf*	daily
1.15	Wonder	Shrewsbury	London	*Plough & Bell*	daily
2.00	Wonder	London	Shrewsbury	*Plough & Bell*	daily
2.45	Tally-ho	London	Birmingham	*Saracen's Head*	daily
3.00	Independent	London	Birmingham		daily
3.15	Crown Prince	London	Birmingham	*Plough & Bell*	daily
3.30	Rising Sun	Cambridge	Birmingham	*Wheat Sheaf*	M., W., F., Sat
4.15	Accommodation	London	Rugby	*Brown Bear*	T., Th., Sat
4.30	Eclipse Tally-ho	London	Birmingham		daily
	NIGHT (pm.)				
10.00pm	Royal Mail	Holyhead	London	*Wheat Sheaf*	daily
11.30	Greyhound	Birmingham	London	*Dun Cow*	daily
12.00	Albion	Birmingham	London	*Brown Bear*	daily
12.00	Emerald	Birmingham	London		daily

Daily mail and stage coaches through Daventry in 1830. (Source: *Pigot & Co's Directory for Northamptonshire*, 1830)

involved not only making an almost entirely new road through North Wales from Shrewsbury, but also improving the road from London to Shropshire. At his insistence, certain turnpike trusts were to be subsidised to give him full control of the project. One of these was the Old Stratford to Dunchurch, to which the Holyhead Road Commissioners paid £5,000 in 1822. Telford's work in shortening distances and levelling gradients can still be seen on the A5 between Towcester and Daventry.

By no means all the traffic which passed through Daventry at this time was bound for Ireland. With the growth of industry in the West Midlands and in Lancashire, the flow between Birmingham, Liverpool and the capital increased greatly. And, although the royal mails took an early lead, stage coaches were just as able to take advantage of improved roads and coach design and soon found themselves better able to provide for the growing demand for passenger facilities. Soon there arose the phenomenon of the 'day

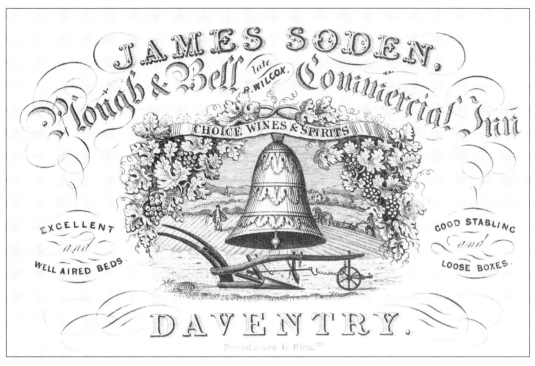

47   *Plough & Bell* billhead. Soden took over from his brother-in-law, Richard Wilcox, in 1843.

coach' to and from London which established itself in most towns on a main road within 140 miles of the capital. Daventry, only half that distance away, was as favourably situated in that respect as it was for the other road developments of the time.

Between 1791 and 1836 the routes of mail and stage coaches through Daventry underwent considerable changes. In 1791 the principal long distance route was from London to Liverpool. Each day the mails made their call at the *Wheat Sheaf* for new horses and a quick bite of refreshment for the passengers. There was also a daily coach on that route—the Liverpool Heavy Coach—which stopped at the *Horse Shoe*. Also passing through three times a week were long distance coaches to London, the Chester Heavy Coach calling at the *Plough and Bell*, the Shrewsbury Heavy Coach at the *Old Quart Pot* and the Coventry Heavy Coach at the *Horse Shoe*. In addition to these a faster day coach between London and Birmingham—the Birmingham Balloon Light Coach—had appeared by 1791: it stopped at the *Wagon and Horses*. Later that year, in competition with it, the proprietors of the Old

Birmingham Balloon Coach announced that a thrice-weekly coach of theirs was to be put on the road between Daventry and London. At that time the only cross-country route through Daventry then served by a regular stage coach was between Birmingham and Cambridge.[2]

About forty years later, in 1830, the pattern had changed considerably. The mails from Liverpool still called at the *Wheat Sheaf* daily, but now Irish mail coaches to and from Holyhead came through. In the 1820s the old Shrewsbury mail had been transformed into the Holyhead mail, and its old route through Oxford was changed to one *via* Daventry and Coventry. At the same time the Chester mail ceased to carry Holyhead traffic. Compared with 1791, the number of long distance passenger coaches passing through in 1830 had only increased from two to three. However, they were now faster and more frequent. Each day to and from Liverpool ran the Express and the Standard, and the Wonder plied daily between London and Shrewsbury. The latter was the most famous coach of its time. It set the fashion for swift long-distance travel, being the first ever to cover much above a

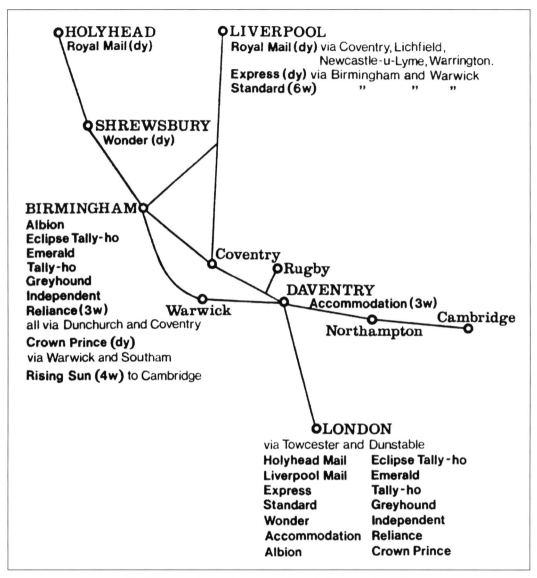

48   Diagram of coaching routes through Daventry in 1830.

hundred miles a day. Great rivalry developed between the fast day coaches and the mails, which had hitherto reigned supreme. The result was some long-remembered 'races' and a general shaving of the time spent on certain journeys. By the early 1830s the mails were reaching Holyhead in 28 hours, the time taken to reach Shrewsbury only a few years before.[3]

Another noticeable feature, comparing 1791 with 1830, is the rise of the fast day coaches between Birmingham and London in the 1820s.

By 1830 no less than seven ran daily, including the Tally-ho and the Eclipse Tally-ho. These were among the fastest in England. Bearing similar names, a typical competitive ruse, they were timed at ten miles an hour, but when 'racing' they went considerably faster. In addition, out of Birmingham there was the Reliance. Two other coaches through Daventry complete the picture for 1830. By that date the Birmingham Light Coach had been replaced by the Rising Sun, and there was the local coach to London, the

49   Bottom of Sheaf Street, looking down Brook End, about 1900. The *Saracen's Head*, with its sign is on the left, centre of the photograph.

Accommodation. It started in 1803 and by 1830 was taking 12 hours to do the journey.[4]

By 1836, when the coaching system reached its acme of perfection, the pattern had changed only a little. The Holyhead and Liverpool mails still ran through the town, and there were still two coaches a day from Liverpool. However, there were now two Manchester coaches—the Red Rover, which got to London in 20 hours, and the Beehive, which took half an hour longer. In the six years since 1830, the Shrewsbury fast coaches had increased to three, the Wonder now being rivalled by the Stage and the Nimrod. Cut-throat competition for passengers, improved road surfaces and lighter, better sprung coaches reduced journey times. The Wonder, doing the run from Shrewsbury to London in a remarkable 15¾ hours, was still the fastest coach in the world, though only 15 minutes faster than the Stage or Nimrod. By 1836 there were six coaches up and down from Birmingham and the two Tally-hos were still the fastest (taking 11¾ hours). The plodding Eclipse took 14.

Another noticeable feature of the 1830s was the growth of short distance coaching. By 1836 there was a coach six times a week between Daventry and Rugby (perhaps because of railway construction business), one four times a week between Daventry and Northampton, and a weekly service between Daventry and Coventry. The Accommodation still ran thrice weekly to London, but never became a fast coach: in 1836 it was still taking as long as in 1791. Finally, the Birmingham to Cambridge coach still ran through Daventry.[5]

It is now difficult to imagine Daventry as a bustling road town. Yet, in 1830 it was remarked that 'the number of coaches passing through were never so great, being 252 weekly, many of which were performing the distance from Daventry to London, 72 miles, in seven hours and three quarters. The above facts, with others that might be noticed, serve to make Daventry one of the most interesting, lively, and inviting towns of its size in the Kingdom'.[6] The development of way-faring benefited Daventry materially. The business brought to local horsedealers, fodder suppliers, innkeepers and publicans, coach proprietors, smiths and farriers, saddlers, harness and whip makers, and the array of journeymen and servants

50 Billhead, the *Saracen's Head*, 1830s. William Buston was landlord from 1831 to 1841, when he moved to the nearby *Crown* commercial inn.

51 The *Bear* inn, High Street, about 1900.

52   The yard of the *Bear*, 1930s.

they employed was more significant in the town's economy than at any time before. Moreover, they were accompanied by new economic developments which seemed to offer a new path for Daventry's future.

The rise of the Footware industry

Shoemaking had been Daventry's main craft since the 16th century and maybe earlier. In the main it had supplied local needs. At the very end of the 18th century there arose in Daventry the industry of making footware for wholesale distribution. Its introduction can be dated with some precision. In 1799 an advertisement appeared offering work 'to real good

hands, in all the various Branches of Men's work'. It was placed by Clarke Gawthorn, a London master.[7] Gawthorn took up his freedom in Daventry the same year and in moving part of his business out into the country was doing what other London masters were doing. The main reasons were the big orders being placed with them for footware for the armed forces and their need to widen their sources of supply. It was this which began the spread of the trade into towns and villages outside

53   Waterloo, from St James Street, about 1900.

Northampton. Other factors were that labour was cheaper and unorganised compared to London, and that, with the opening of the Grand Junction Canal, communications had improved. Although the branch to Daventry provided for in the Act of 1793 was never constructed, the canal wharves at Braunston and Long Buckby were within reach, and the canal itself passed through the northern edge of the parish, or, more accurately, passed under it through the Braunston tunnel, completed in 1796. Gawthorn was soon joined in the wholesale trade by another manufacturer, William Lee, a local man who took up his freedom in 1800. By 1830 there were six small firms. Eleven years later there were nine giving work to 443 workers, shoemakers now being almost ten per cent of Daventry's population.[8] It must have seemed that Daventry was looking at a manufacturing future.

In this period Daventry's population, like that of virtually every other place in the county, was on the increase, rising from 2,582 in 1801 to 4,565 in 1841. The first phase of town expansion, particularly for the housing of the poor, consisted of filling existing spaces, with the building of

54   Rose Court, Brook Street, about 1900.

'courts' in the gardens of town houses and the yards of inns. In Daventry these were to be found in Brook Street (the old 'Brook End' of town), Abbey Street (the old 'Abbey End') and behind the west side of Sheaf Street. In 1851 the courts in this latter place were Prince Regent Court, Wagon Court, Black Boy Court, St James Court and Rose Court. The lane behind was eventually laid out as George Street, its continuation across Tavern Lane becoming known as Waterloo. By 1851 George Street had been re-named St James Street. This was the district where the shoemakers lived. Behind the terraced houses on the west side of St James Street brick-built shops were erected where they did their daily 'stabbing and stitching'.

Religion and education from 1790 to 1840

Amongst the changes affecting society in the later 18th century was the rise of 'Vital Religion'. The desire on the part of evangelicals to promote more active and zealous forms of christianity affected both the Church and Dissent, but one of its most important developments was the rise of Methodism. Its mission was to carry the gospel to people others were failing to reach. They first appeared in the district in 1788 when a 'society' of four persons began to meet at Norton. By 1797 their numbers had grown and they started to meet in a room in Daventry. In 1801 they moved to a meeting house in Chapel Lane, finally opening a purpose-built chapel in Cow Lane in 1824.[9] This became the centre of the Daventry and Rugby circuit, which comprised 23 societies served by three ministers. However, not even the Wesleyans could avoid the system of pew appropriation. Income for chapel maintenance and the payment of ministers had to be raised from the rent of sittings. At the time of the Religious Census of 1851 only about a third of the seats were free.[10] In 1846 the membership of the chapel stood at 126.

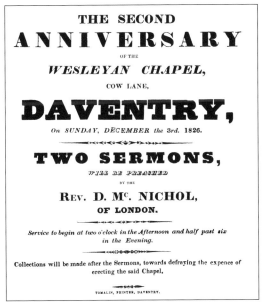

55 Handbill, second anniversary of Daventry Wesleyan chapel, 1826.

If churchmen and Dissenters found Wesleyan preaching and practices vulgar, they could not ignore the success of their appeal nor let their ideas and institutions go unrivalled. An equally important factor in the Evangelical Revival was the fear of the spread of 'infidelity' as a consequence of the French Revolution. In 1812 the Independents started a Bible Association in Daventry 'for the purpose of disseminating the Holy Scriptures among the Poor'. Three years later a local Auxiliary of the Society for the Propagation of Religious Knowledge, a church body, was formed, the function of which was the sale of bibles and religious literature to subscribers for distribution among their servants and the poor of the district.[11] In these years Church and Chapel followed the example of the Wesleyans and became involved in the running of Sunday Schools. The Sheaf Street Chapel School was founded by the daughter of the Rev. George Watson, minister there from 1799 to 1816. In 1812 the Rev. Sir John Knightley left a bequest to pay for a church Sunday School. By the time Queen Victoria came to the throne hundreds of children were attending Daventry's Sunday Schools, and of all the religious institutions of her reign it would be hard to think of a more characteristic one. Independents and Wesleyans put a greater

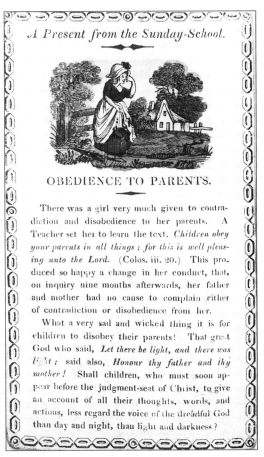

56 Early Victorian homily card from the Independent Chapel Sunday School.

emphasis on Sunday Schools than the Church of England, which saw its role more as a provider of day schools.

In the early 19th century it was apparent, with a growing population, that there were gaps in the existing provision. In 1826 a National (Church) School was opened, which absorbed the old English Charity School. The 24 'foundation boys' continued to be educated and clothed from the old endowment, but by 1841 another 116 were being educated in the school, which was maintained by voluntary subscriptions, the support of the National Society and a small government grant. In 1826 the school was moved into the rebuilt Abbey buildings, where, with grim inappropriateness, it was housed close by the poor-house and town gaol.[12] In 1829 the corporation made a loan, raised by the sale of

57 Daventry church and the Priory buildings, shortly before the demolition and rebuilding of the latter as a school, gaol and poorhouse, 1826.

timber on the Cosford estate, to the trustees of the English Charity School to build and establish a school 'for the education of all the poor girls within the parish of Daventry'.[13] However, there were only 12 in it in 1841.

These developments were accompanied by growing denominational rivalry. Increasingly, Dissenters viewed the virtual monopoly of the Church over education as a challenge. During the pastorate at Sheaf Street of the vigorous Rev.

John Davies (1826-57) it was decided to re-found a day school of their own. Funds were raised to establish a school on the principles of the British and Foreign Schools Society, the rival body to the Church's National Society for the Education of the Children of the Poor in the Principles of the Church of England.[14] The opening of the British School in its own premises in 1844 was a great source of satisfaction to Dissenters and Wesleyans. It was to survive until taken over by the Local Education Authority in 1906. Nevertheless, it was smaller than the National School. As in other matters, though the Dissenters were able to oppose the Church and its supporters, they could not outmatch them.

This had been made clear with the opening of Daventry's second church. In 1838 the Peter-borough Diocesan Church Building Association, whose object was to build churches in towns where there were few free seats in existing parish churches, raised the money to open three new churches. Two were in Northampton and the third in Daventry. It was to have 488 seats of which half were to be free.[15] Comparing the money-raising efforts of the Church with those of Dissenters for such projects, the difference is marked. The £2,000 required to build and endow this 'chapel of ease' in Daventry was raised without

58   The new church of St James, *c*.1840.

difficulties and it was opened in a remarkably short time. In July 1840 the Bishop of Peterborough arrived in George Street to consecrate the church of St James, set down in the midst of Daventry's shoe-making population.

By the middle of the 19th century the influence of evangelicalism in Daventry was, as elsewhere, marked. The 'Victorian Sunday' was strongly observed, as were 'Days of Humiliation'. In 1849 to 'atone for' the recent cholera epidemic, seen clearly as punishment visited by a stern deity upon a nation of sinners, a national day of humiliation was called for 5 October. The faithful passed the day in fasting and prayer, shops were closed, and there were services at Holy Cross and St James.[16] There were to be others, over such calamities as the Indian Mutiny and the Crimean War. In the previous six decades or so, vital religion had changed both Dissenters and the Church. In doing so, it widened the sectarian divide. As well as responding to the educational challenge, Dissenters were mounting a political one as well. By 1851 both sides were vigorous and combative, but the findings of the Religious Census of that year clearly show the Church was holding its own. On Census Sunday attenders at Holy Cross and St James were twice as numerous as those at the Independent and Wesleyan chapels combined. The Church's hold on education and the borough charities had not been seriously lessened, and in politics its interests were strongly defended by the forces of Conservatism.

The Corporation, the War and the Daventry Improvement Act

In the 1780s it seemed that the times were favourable to the prospects of the reform of this country's institutions, which had been unmodified for a century. In 1789 Protestant Dissenters from Daventry joined with others in petitioning Parliament for the repeal of the Test Act. Their timing was unlucky. Reform was stopped and then put into sharp reverse by the outbreak of war against Revolutionary France. A patriotic 'King and country' temper manifested itself, and anyone making the slightest criticism of this country's institutions soon found himself regarded as a Jacobin, a republican enemy of the state. It was this temper which led to the sacking of the house in Birmingham of the most distinguished alumnus of Daventry Dissenting Academy, Joseph Priestley, by a 'Church and King' mob in 1791.

DODDRIDGE ACADEMY
JOSEPH PRIESTLEY, L.L.D.,F.R.S.
THEOLOGIAN and MAN of SCIENCE
was a STUDENT here
1752 – 1755

59 Plaque to Joseph Priestley, Sheaf Street, put up in 1934 (L.G. Tooby).

Priestley was singularly fortunate not to have been at home at the time. Loyalty declarations were the order of the day and there was one in Daventry in December 1792. The church bells were tolled, and a crowd paraded the town singing 'God Save the King'. On the market hill an effigy of Thomas Paine, author of *Rights of Man* and a supporter of the American as well as the French Revolutions, was burned.[17] It was a time for Reformers and Dissenters to keep their heads down.

In those years Daventry was the scene of considerable military activity. As always, soldiers and sailors passed through the town and often stopped for quarter. The local troop of the North-amptonshire Yeomanry drilled regularly on Borough Hill, and in 1797 a Volunteer company was raised in Daventry. In the event it never played much of a role in the defence of the realm but it came in useful as an extra arm of the law. The years before and after the turn of the century saw harvest failures, rising food prices and increasing poverty. Fear that economic discontent might combine with sedition put the authorities on the alert. In September 1800, receiving information that 'Several inflammatory and seditious papers' had been posted in the town and having received 'private information of an intended riot in the market', the Bailiff called out the Yeomanry and Volunteers to assist in preserving the peace. The origins of the trouble were revealed as more economic than revolutionary when the Bailiff offered a five pound reward leading to the prosecution of those Georgian social devils, any 'forestaller, ingrosser or regrator' suspected of profiteering in food.[18] The activity of the military became even more prominent in 1803 when the government built an arsenal at Weedon. Located

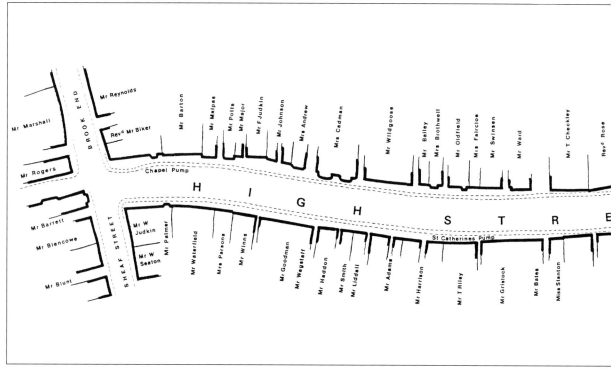

60   Plan of High Street, 1788, made for a proposed paving scheme.

on the Grand Junction canal, it consisted of 12 powder magazines, barracks for two regiments of the line, and three pavilions to which George III planned to retreat if the French landed, Weedon being just about as far from the sea as one could be in the whole of England. One can only suppose the government assumed that, if the French had landed, it would have escaped the notice of their intelligence that Watling Street ran straight up to the royal hideout.

In 1806 another body was added to the local government of Daventry in the form of the Daventry Improvement Commissioners. One reason for acquiring the private Act of Parliament which brought them into existence was that in the later years of the 18th century there grew up the wish to have the streets better paved, drained, lit and cleansed. In 1788 a plan for the improving of High Street was made with detailed provisions for draining, levelling of the gradient in the middle, and the pebbling of the Hog market.[19] The scheme was costly, and though tenders were invited, it is not certain whether it was carried through. In any case, the town authorities decided

to seek extra powers from Parliament to initiate and pay for future schemes. A second reason was the growing popularity of the market and fairs and the need for further powers to regulate them. And last but not least the old Moot Hall had become so dilapidated that it was now unsafe. Legislation was necessary for powers to purchase it from the lord of the manor and raise money to erect or purchase a new one.

Accordingly an Act was secured. Because it was not possible to give more powers to the corporation under its existing charter, a new and separate authority in the form of a body of Improvement Commissioners was created. The Bailiff, Recorder, his deputy and some forty leading figures in the borough were named in the Act as the first body of commissioners.[20] When the time came for their successors to be appointed, Daventry was to keep its close-corporate practice of proposing names of replacements without the bother of elections (as happened in unincorporated towns). Commissioners had to have a fairly high property qualification and, in practice, much the same men who were on the corporation were

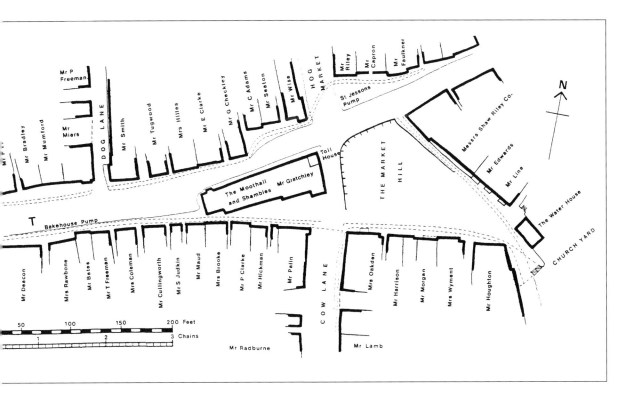

active on that body. They had the power to levy an improvement rate and, armed with the power to borrow money upon the security of the rates, they set to work to improve Daventry.

For the first time the streets were cleaned on a regular basis. They took action against perpetrators of 'offensive nuisances'. They planned to repair the pavements, though for years fear of the cost of a major paving and draining programme delayed implementation. In the early days the commissioners had a long struggle to make shopkeepers and licensees remove their sign posts and stalls from the pavements. Another important task was to improve the lighting of the town. In 1806 there were a few oil lamps and the numbers were increased, though at 2s. 8d. a gallon (in 1829) 'best pale seal oil' was expensive. The commissioners were relieved when in 1833 the lighting of the town was handed over to the newly formed gas company, though they still had to pay the lighting bill. On the matter of watching the commissioners moved slowly. It was not until 1830 that the vestry decided to appoint a 'street keeper' or beadle, the commissioners contributing £10 a

year to his salary. His duties were to patrol the town from 9.00 a.m. until midnight with the special task of moving on beggars. He was also to prevent boys playing in the street and was required to keep an eye on public houses at night. Cooperation between the vestry and the commissioners over this was short-lived. In 1832 the latter recorded their opinion that the employment of a watchman was useless and refused to contribute further towards this post. The beadle therefore reverted to being an official of the vestry.[21]

A second function of the commissioners was to remake the bye-laws for the better regulation of the market and fairs. A first task was to divide and re-locate the different parts of the market. In 1806 they decided that from then on butchers' meat should only be sold on the site of the old butchers' Shambles and Moot Hall. Cheese should only be sold on the market hill and the site of the Moot Hall. Sheep and lambs were to be sold only in High Street, and rams and tups on the south side of the market hill. Oxen, cows and neat cattle were to be sold only in Cow Lane, Badby Road, the west end of Tavern Lane and

DAVENTRY MICHAELMAS FAIR.

AT a Meeting of the Commissioners, held at the Moot-Hall, in DAVENTRY, on the 31st of August, 1809, appointed by an Act of Parliament passed in the 46th Year of his present Majesty's Reign, intitled, " An Act for Paving, Cleansing, Lighting, and Watching the Town of Daventry, in the County of Northampton, and for regulating the Market there; and for enabling the Bailiff, Burgesses, and Commonalty of the Borough of Daventry to purchase the Moot-Hall, and rebuild the same;"

It was ordered, That the following Rules, Orders, and By-laws, for regulating the MICHAELMAS FAIR, at DAVENTRY, and the several Persons resorting thereto, to be made and established:—

It was ordered, directed, and appointed, That for the greater Accommodation of Persons resorting to the Michaelmas Fair, and to prevent Accidents and Inconvenience from the Streets of Daventry being too much crowded, that yearly and every Year the 2d Day of October, being the first Day of the said Michaelmas Fair, be appropriated for the Sale, and exposing to Sale, of Cheese, Onions, and all Sorts of Wares and Merchandise; and that no Beasts, Sheep, Horses, or other Cattle should thereafter be sold or exposed to Sale on the said 2d Day of October in the Parish of Daventry, on Pain for every Person offending forfeiting the Sum of Twenty Shillings for every Offence.

It was further ordered, That the 3d Day of October, being the second Day of Michaelmas Fair, should yearly and every Year be appropriated to the Sale, and exposing to Sale, of all Sorts of Beasts, Horses, Sheep, and other Cattle. By Order of the said Commissioners,

EDM. BURTON.

Daventry, September 14th, 1810.

61 Improvement Commissioners' notice about Michaelmas Fair in the *Northampton Mercury*, 1810.

Staverton Road, all well away from the market place and High Street. They also specified the precise areas of pavement in High Street on which butter, eggs, poultry, fruit and vegetables were to be sold. In addition, strict traffic routes for wagons and carts coming into town on market and fair days were laid down. There were also changes in the timing and numbers of fairs and the market. From 1808 it was decided that the weekly corn market was not to commence before 11.00 a.m., nor continue after 1.00p.m. From 1809, to prevent inconvenience from the streets being too crowded, the first day of Michaelmas Fair was reserved for the sale of cheese and onions and all sorts of wares and merchandise. No livestock was to be allowed until the second day. Because of the growth of business, in 1806 three new cattle fairs were added to the Daventry calendar, and another one in 1825.[22] Another amended list of fairs was published in 1835, by which time the number had grown to 12 fairs. By 1856 there were 14 fairs.

The third objective of the Improvement Act was the purchase and replacement of the Moot Hall. A price was agreed between the corporation and the lord of the manor for the building, its site and the market tolls belonging to it, and the old Moot Hall was duly purchased and demolished. A house in the Hog Market belonging to Mr. Watkins was purchased and was soon in use as the new Moot Hall. The cost of these transactions, and the Act of Parliament needed to sanction them, came to over £2,000, a very large sum for such a small borough as Daventry. The raising of the necessary finances and ramifications over the lease of the building became so complicated that, 70 years later, a special committee of inquiry had to be instituted to sort them out. It did not prove easy.

As we have already seen, the cost of poor relief in Daventry grew markedly between the 1790s and 1830. There were several reasons for this, not all of which were understood at the time. From about 1760 the population of Daventry (and everywhere else) was increasing but, in the absence of any form of local or national population count before the census of 1801, the importance of this was not appreciated. There were also factors at work, particularly the long wars against the French which distorted the economy, and a series of bad harvests pushed up the price of bread to unprecedented heights. Because farming and those involved in agricultural business generally did well in the wars, the rising cost of poor relief did not upset the ratepayers too much. The ending of the wars, however, brought a serious depression in farming and in 1817-19 the poor rates rose higher than ever before, causing growing concern. In the first 20 years of the 19th century Daventry's population grew by a further 30 per cent and there was a corresponding increase in the amount expended on the poor. Although this alarmed the vestry and parish officials, Daventry fared rather better than some neighbouring parishes, partly because it had no old industries which had collapsed, such as lace at Towcester or woolcombing and weaving at Long Buckby, and partly because in those 20 years the shoe trade was beginning to provide work locally. Nonetheless, the burden of poor relief weighed heavily on the authorities, the tax payers and of course the poor who in these years went through great privation.

The parish authorities did what all authorities were doing at the time. They moved on vagrants, the tramping unemployed and the steady stream of crippled soldiers and sailors. They tried to run the poor house at Brook End economically. They considered setting up a 'house of industry' to employ the able-bodied. In the end, in 1824 they purchased the old Abbey Buildings and converted them into a workhouse, gaol and school, and for the next 14 years used the workhouse part to house the poor. They also adopted the system whereby a Select Vestry took over the administration of poor relief. It was hoped that the Select, whose membership was restricted to the richer ratepayers, by meeting more regularly could exercise a more businesslike and economical control on spending than the Vestry, the current wisdom being that the old system of parish relief was shot through with administrative abuses. The minute book of the Daventry Select Vestry for the years 1819 to 1835 shows that it handled the difficult problem of poor relief in much the same ways as the Vestry had done.[23] In the end a new system came along in the 1830s which transferred most of the responsibility for poor relief to poor law unions, boards of guardians and new-style workhouses, as we shall see.

Another development of these years was the formation of the Daventry District Association for the Prosecution of Crimes. An increase in rural crime from about 1780 exposed weaknesses in the old system of pursuit by parish constable, and the leaving of the prosecution of suspected offenders largely to individual initiative. In 1783 a meeting was called in Daventry to promote a society for prosecuting persons suspected of robberies, burglaries and horse- and sheep-stealing in the counties of Northamptonshire and Warwickshire.[24] Such bodies were being set up in many places, but the Daventry initiative came to nothing until 1817. The Association existed to take action if one of its members suffered from such crimes. Although there is no reason to suspect that their efforts were crowned with notable triumphs of thief-taking, they acted as a deterrent and a supplement to the efforts of parish constables and magistrates. In retrospect, they were an interim device in an era which was very suspicious of the idea of a regular police force, the latter not appearing until 1839.

Daventry and the coming of Reform

In the 'Old Tory' atmosphere of post-war Daventry the ideas of Reform—representative government, religious liberty, and the liberalisation of economic life—were slow to emerge. They

DAVENTRY OLD BANK.

We, the Undersigned, being perfectly satisfied of the responsibility of the House of Messrs. **WATKINS & SON**, do hereby declare that we are willing to accept their Notes in payment to any amount, and that we will support the **BANK** to the utmost of our power.

CHARLES KNIGHTLEY.	JOSEPH CASTELL,
Wм. SAWBRIDGE,	T. BATES & SONS,
CHARLES RATTRAY,	T. POTTS,
R. TAWNEY, *Dunchurch*.	W. & B. DUNKLEY,
W. R. ROSE,	J BROMWICH,
R. H. LAMB,	W. SLATCHER,
J. P. CLARKE,	M. MILLER,
E. S. BURTON,	W. CRANE,
THOMAS NEWMAN, *Braunston.*	W. BUTLIN,
T. HOWES, *Norton*,	T. WEST,
J. WILLIAMS,	T. FAULKNER,
WALL & DANIEL,	W. KENDRICK,
C. CORRALL,	B. W. PALMER,
THOMAS DUNKLEY,	T. MARFELL,
JAMES BLISS,	J. HANDS, *Preston*,
JOHN MOLLADY,	J. MANN,
MARY TOMALIN,	R. WEBB,
C. GAWTHORN,	E. MAUD,
G. MARRIOTT,	A. WILKINS & SON,
JOHN BLENCOWE,	W. BUCKNELL,
W. MORTON,	W. PETTIFER,
R. COLE,	T. C. PHILLIPS,
W. CARR,	W. EDMUNDS, *Thrupp*,

Daventry, 17th. December, 1825.

Tomalin, Printer, Market Place, Daventry.

62   Handbill, 1825 bank crisis.

began to do so in 1825, which in several ways was a year of crisis. A serious harvest failure precipitated an economic recession. A crisis of confidence plunged a large number of country banks into serious trouble. One such was the 'Daventry Old Bank' of Watkins & Son, which was in danger of collapse, with all that meant for local people and businesses, when the bank in London which discounted its bills suspended payments. After a short but very serious panic, public confidence was re-established and arrangements made with another London bank to have Daventry notes paid there. The recession, however, proved to be serious. Unemployment and poor relief matters took centre stage. Radical Reformers argued that the economic policies of Toryism were in large

DAVENTRY
OLD BANK.

In consequence of Messrs. SIKES, SNAITH, & Co. having suspended their Payments, Messrs. WATKINS & SON have made arrangements to have their Notes paid by Sir Richard Carr GLYN and Co.

22nd. December, 1825.

TOM .IN, PRINTER, MARKET PLACE, DAVENTRY.

63   Handbill, the 1825 bank crisis averted.

measure to blame for the situation and pressure for reform began to mount. One local aspect of this was the Dickins affair.

From time to time in the deliberations of the corporation the question of the maintaining the old regulations about taking up freedoms was raised. The matter had not come up for some time when, in 1824, the corporation found that 63 traders and craftsmen were carrying on business without having gone through this formality. When pressed, most did so, but John Dickins, whipmaker, refused, and in due course the town clerk was instructed to take proceedings against him. An action was brought at the Lent Assizes the next year and the verdict went to the plaintiffs, with costs of 40 shillings. Dickins had the case re-opened on a technicality. At the new trial the case for the corporation was that it was 'an ancient and laudable custom' of Daventry that every person should purchase his freedom before being allowed to practise his trade there, and damages of £500 against Dickins were sought.

Counsel for Dickins argued that no charter could impose such rules, and that without an Act of Parliament no person could be so restrained. He also argued that there were, as the plaintiffs admitted, exceptions to the rule: women, poor tradesmen and traders at the markets and fairs were all exempt. However, the verdict went to the corporation, though the damages they were awarded, one farthing, were derisory.[25]

Dickins took this as a moral victory and persisted in his refusal. The next we hear of the matter is his indictment for composing a defamatory libel in the form of *A Letter Addressed to 'J.W.'* [John Wildgoose] in 1826. This action went against Dickins, because, in November that year, the Bailiff and burgesses ordered that 'it be intimated to John Dickins that unless he agrees to the proposition made to him for his liberation from Gaol on or before the seventh day of December these terms will not be thereafter accepted'.[26] Precisely what these terms were is not certain, but Dickins must have agreed because

THE INHABITANTS OF DAVENTRY,

Friendly to Religious Toleration,

ARE RESPECTFULLY INVITED TO ATTEND A

PUBLIC

MEETING,

AT THE

Saracen's Head Inn,

On FRIDAY EVENING NEXT,

To consider the propriety of Petitioning Parliament in furtherance of **CATHOLIC EMANCIPATION**, and also of expressing their gratitude to His Majesty's Ministers, for their present dignified and impartial measures.

The Chair will be taken at seven o'clock.

23rd. FEB. 1829.

Tomalin, Printer, Daventry.

64 Handbill issued by Reformers, 1829. Ordered by Thomas Dickins.

he was released from prison. However, as late as 1831 he was still delaying. In the end, in the face of another threat of legal action, he gave in, finally taking up his freedom in May 1832.

This storm in a Daventry tea-cup was perhaps of wider importance. Making due allowance that Dickins was an awkward party who enjoyed martyrdom, his battle was over free enterprise being allowed to break out of old corporate restrictions, upheld in places old-fashioned enough not to see the way economic ideas was moving. Others were ignoring old rules about taking up freedoms, but not Daventry. Dickins, a Dissenter, was fighting the liberal corner. Perhaps he dragged out his case because in those years Reform was on the move. In 1828 Dissenters made their political break-though with the repeal of the Test and Corporation Acts, and Catholic Emancipation followed a year later. Two years later the biggest political crisis of the whole 19th century blew up over the question of modernising the old political system put in place in 1689. It coincided with the onset of another economic depression, large-scale industrial unrest, soaring poor rates, a famine in Ireland, a revolution in France and the visitation of the cholera in England.

The crisis began in March 1831. When Daventry reformers petitioned the Tory Bailiff, Dr. Rattray, to call a meeting of inhabitants in the Moot Hall, he was obstructive. They were obliged to meet in the *Saracen's Head*. The chair was taken by the Whig solicitor, Thomas Orton Gery, and the meeting resolved to send petitions in favour of Reform to both houses of Parliament.[27] When the Lords rejected the first Reform Bill a general election was called. All over the country the contest was excited and bitterly fought. In Northamptonshire its result was a tremendous blow to Toryism. Since 1806 there had not been a contested election for the two county seats, and the squires who dominated

TO THE
Boroughmongers.

YOUR Reign is past, the glorious fight is won!
In vain you strive,—REFORM'S full tide rolls on;
As o'er the Land like some vast flood it flows,
Strong from a thousand generous springs it grows.
RETIRE IN TIME!!! before its awful force,
Nor trust to feeble B——s to stop its course.

TOMALIN, PRINTER, DAVENTRY.

65 Reform handbill at the time of the Reform Election, 1831. 'Feeble B—s' almost certainly refers to the Burtons.

politics had got used to a comfortable and inexpensive arrangement whereby the Whig, Lord Althorp, and the Tory, William Ralph Cartwright of Aynho, were returned unopposed. This arrangement was shattered in 1831 when Lord Milton, son of Earl Fitzwilliam, a Whig grandee, intervened, and forced a contest. This resulted in the defeat of both Cartwright and his Tory running-mate, Sir Charles Knightley.

The result was a shock to Tory Daventry, whose leading figures were passionate in their support for Cartwright and Knightley. They cheered themselves up by organising a great dinner in which the two candidates were fêted as splendidly as if they had won.[28] Prominent in the arrangements was Daventry Toryism's most influential figure, Edmund Singer Burton, the town clerk, the second of a dynasty who held that position for a century. The first was his father, Edmund Burton (1760 to 1820), whom he

succeeded on the latter's death. After his death in 1863, E.S. Burton was followed in turn by his son, Edmund Charles, a memorial to whom stands facing the Moot Hall. As lawyers in private practice, town clerks, stewards to the manorial court, clerks to the Improvement Commissioners and the turnpike trust, and as political agents to Tory candidates in many elections, there was little in the public life of Daventry and district in which they were not involved.

Although within a short time local Tories regained their grip, there was little they could do to stem the flood of Reform. In that momentous year, 1831-2, events moved rapidly towards a crisis. When the Lords threw out the second Reform Bill in October there was rioting in several cities, notably in Bristol and Nottingham. At Weedon Royal Arsenal orders were issued to put into an efficient state of defence the vast magazines of gun-powder and other war stores. A few weeks later it was reported that the barracks were 'literally crammed with troops'.[29] In the event there was no uprising, but unrest did not end until the final crisis of April to June 1832. Then, the House of Lords, faced with the threat by the king to swamp them with newly-created Whig peers, capitulated and allowed the third Reform Bill to pass into law. High Tory squires such as the Cartwrights, Knightleys, Thorntons and Drydens bemoaned the passing of England's 'matchless' constitution, but were soon to find that, for them, the implications were anything but radical. Indeed, instead of having two seats for the county, Northamptonshire now had four, two each for the new North and South divisions, and the recovery of the Tory party began right away in the election of December 1832. In South Northamptonshire, the old agreement of Lord Althorp and W.R. Cartwright being returned without a contest was re-made, and by 1835 the Whigs had been ousted from both county seats. It almost seemed by then that the Reform Act had never happened.

The new political era had less comfortable consequences for Daventry. Now a polling place for the southern division, whenever parliamentary elections were called, the political circus came to town. Between then and 1872, when the ballot made elections altogether quieter, there were many boisterous scenes at the hustings. More sober consequences followed as a result of other Whig reforms in the 1830s. The first of these was the Poor Law Amendment Act of 1834. This removed the relief of the poor from the individual parish, where it had been exercised since Elizabethan times, and gave it to a new body. This was the poor law union, made by combining groups of parishes. The Daventry union consisted of Daventry and 27 surrounding parishes. The Act made it a condition that relief would only be given in the union workhouse. This was to be managed in such a way that only people in 'genuine' poverty would apply. According to its architects, 'malingerers' would be removed from the system. Management of each union was to be by a board of guardians, elected by the parish ratepayers, and in 1840 the new union workhouse (the Danetre Hospital of the 20th century) was opened to the south of the town, on London Road. Apart from its many consequences for the poor and the ratepayers, the 1834 Act was a blow to parish government. From then on, the vestry began to wither, its

remaining functions eventually passing to other authorities.

In 1835 the Municipal Corporations Act, a local government counterpart to parliamentary reform, came on to the Statute book. The object was to abolish the close-corporations of 178 ancient boroughs, of which Daventry was one, and replace them with municipal councils elected by and responsible to the ratepayers. The expectation was that, when a more representative system of town government was instituted, the self-perpetuating Tory oligarchies would be replaced by councils more closely representing the opinions of the ratepayers. In some places this led to a revolution in the town hall. But not in Daventry. At the first municipal election in December 1835, nine of the 12 councillors were former corporation burgesses, and all were Tories.[30] Of the three Whigs, one, Charles Bliss, a draper, had been one of the commonalty. The other two, Thomas Lee and Joseph Billingham, both shoe-manufacturers, were the only new blood. The first four aldermen were also Tories. The result reflected the strength of Toryism and the shortage of Whigs and Dissenters on the ground. Subsequent municipal contests only emphasised this, and soon the whole council was Tory. When vacancies occurred in the next few years, seats were invariably filled by men of that party. Two other effects of the new arrangements should be noted. The geographical area of the municipal borough was altered. Since 1676 it had been co-terminous with the parish. From 1835 it was reduced to the town of Daventry and the hamlet of Drayton, most of the farms and farmland now being outside the municipality. And from that year the custom and practice of compelling people who wanted to set up in business in Daventry to take up their freedom was consigned to the dustbin of history. Dickins had won.

Administratively, the replacement of the corporation by the council made scarcely any difference. George Mallaber, Bailiff in 1833-4, became Daventry's first mayor, and E.S. Burton was appointed town clerk. A mortgage on the security of the Moot Hall, 10 Moot Hall shares and the two silver maces were inherited from the corporation, and there was some uncertainty about the new council's position in these matters. Legal opinion was sought as to whether the new authority had the right to use the Moot

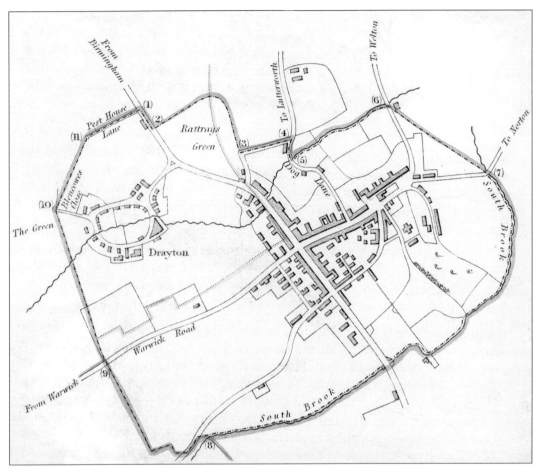

66   The reduced bounds of Daventry borough in 1835.

67   The sign of mayoral authority: believed to be William Collins, Mayor's Sergeant, 1885 to 1916.

Hall. It was confirmed that it had, but the 10 shares were ordered to be sold by public auction. The first years of municipal government were intended by the government to be plain and economical to mark a contrast with the ceremonial and 'feasting' of the old corporations. The office of sergeant-at-mace was abolished, and in 1851 the lesser mace was presented to Henry Barne Sawbridge as a token of respect and an acknowledgement of the charities founded by his forebears. In fact, only a few years later, all this was reversed. A Mayor's sergeant was appointed, the great mace was carried once more, and the Sawbridge family returned the lesser mace. There was also a confused hiatus in the matter of the old corporation charities. It was found that the council could not inherit the role of the old corporation and, as we have seen, the

Charity Commissioners came up with a new scheme.

Daventry and the coming of the railway

If old Daventry was able to ride out the challenge of political reform, it could not do the same with another and far more threatening danger which emerged at almost exactly the same time—the railway. The year 1830 saw the formation of the first and most important of the Midland, and indeed national, railway companies, the London & Birmingham. The danger to business in road towns was seen immediately. At a meeting in Towcester in January 1831 a committee was formed to oppose the London & Birmingham Bill in Parliament, which included such local landowners as Sir William Wake, Sir Charles Knightley, Thomas Reeve Thornton and Edward Bouverie of Delapre Abbey, with E.S. Burton as their solicitor and agent. Another source of opposition came from the trustees of the Old Stratford to Dunchurch Turnpike Trust. Worried about their investments, they also formed another committee to oppose the Bill. The likely consequences of the railway were outlined in an anonymous pamphlet from Daventry. It predicted the ruin both of the canal and long-distance goods and passenger traffic on the roads, with the most deleterious effects on towns such as Daventry and Towcester. It also predicted disaster for the breeders and suppliers of the estimated million horses engaged on the national roads at that time and for suppliers of fodder, it being calculated that horses then consumed a third of the amount of foodstuffs consumed by people. It also outlined the threat to innkeepers, servants and craftsmen whose livelihoods were involved with road business.[31]

Although the suggestion would have been anathema to the author of the pamphlet, Daventry's best hope for the future was that the railway would pass through it. Unfortunately, because of its hilly topography, the plans for the railway by-passed the town. That was understood by the pro-Railway lobby in Daventry from the outset. However, its committee, upon which the local shoe manufacturers and John Dickins figured prominently, made great efforts to persuade the London & Birmingham Company to build a branch line into Daventry.[32] To the extent that the branch line was included in the Bill eventually passed in Parliament, their efforts were successful.

68 Handbill on the prospect of the London & Birmingham Railway.

In the event, it was never built, just as the promised branch line of the Grand Junction Canal had never materialised in an earlier part of the transport revolution.

The political struggle over the London & Birmingham Bill took place at the same time as the Reform crisis. In November the Company deposited plans with the Board of Trade and the county authorities. The following April the bill reached committee stage and something of a furore was caused when the House of Lords rejected it. For a time it seemed as though the landed interest had defeated the powerful railway lobby. However, money talked. The opposition was bought off with generous compensation for owners of land over which the railway was to run. The new Bill received the royal assent on 6 May 1833, and just over a year later construction work started.

The local effects of the opening of the railway in September 1838 were immediate and serious.

69   After the railway the roads went quiet. London Road, about 1900. The *Wheat Sheaf* stands at the top of the road.

Right away, canal boatmen were laid off. As early as the first week in October the number of coaches travelling daily through Daventry between London and Birmingham went down from 20 to five, and notices of the sale of coaches as famous as the Wonder and the Swallow soon appeared in the newspapers. The following year, tolls on the Old Stratford to Dunchurch turnpike were down by 50 per cent, compared with 1834.[33] The coaching era had come to an abrupt end and the once-busy national route which had been the basis of Daventry's importance since the time of Queen Elizabeth emptied of traffic. Its inns fell on hard times. When Benjamin Wyment Palmer became landlord of the *Wheat Sheaf* in 1841 he entered with the usual flourish. Once, to have taken the *Wheat Sheaf* was to have acquired the premier position in the licensed trade in Daventry. Not any more. By 1845 he was in financial difficulties

and two years later and collapsed into bankruptcy. Its post-horses, flys, gigs, phaeton, chariot hearse, and harnesses; the stock-in-trade and wines; the furniture of the drawing room, the six sitting-rooms and the 14 bedrooms, with the cut glass and dinner services; the contents of the kitchens; all came under the hammer.[34]

'This the principal inn in this place', declared the *Northampton Herald*, 'and for many years one of the first commercial and posting houses between London and Liverpool, is now closed for want of a tenant'. A proposal to use it for 'Northampton-shire College', a new public school, came to nothing.[35] When it re-opened it was not as an inn and posting house, but as a public house and a commercial hotel, a mere shadow of its former glory. And Victorian Daventry was destined to be a mere shadow of its Georgian glory.

Eight

The Long Decline:
Victorian Daventry 1840 to 1900

Steady-state economics

After the opening of the London & Birmingham Railway the town entered upon a decline which was to last for over a hundred years. Nothing records this more graphically than the census returns. From its peak in 1841, Daventry's population declined decade by decade until it reached its lowest point just before the First World War (the only exception to this trend being in 1891, when the temporary presence of railway workers boosted the figure). In these 70 years its population fell overall by about one thousand. Daventry had become Sleepy Hollow. And for another half century it remained Sleepy Hollow: it was not until the 1950s that its population reached the level it had been at in 1841.

Though hopes were raised in 1845, 1858 and 1864, the railway did not arrive in Daventry from Weedon until 1888. It brought some benefits, but as a branch line it made little difference to the economic prospects of the town. Nor did the connection with Leamington in 1895. Daventry was not unique; the failure of the railway to arrive early put many a town to sleep. There were perhaps other reasons. Daventry's failure to compensate for this setback owed much to its economic conservatism, well-illustrated by the Dickins case. The élite in the Moot Hall loved trade, admired the professions but despised industry, regarding manufacturers with considerable disdain. Victorian Daventry's Tories took a pride in keeping Whigs, Liberals and

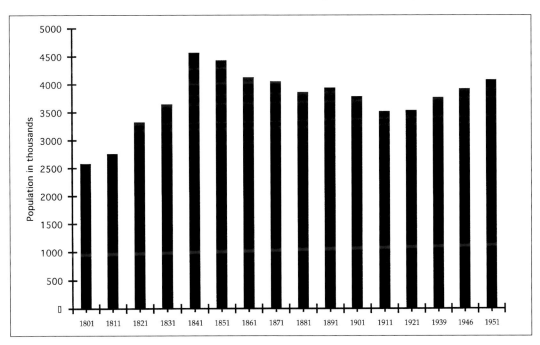

70 Population graph, 1801 to 1951.

To the FRIENDS of the LABOURING
MANUFACTURER.

A

Case of Benevolence.

The Public are respectfully informed, that, in consideration
of the *reasonableness* of the advance in the price of labor,
which is at the present solicited by the operative Boot and
Shoe Makers, and the *distress* in which many are involved
in consequence of the measure to which they have *neces-*
sarily been obliged to have recourse in order to obtain a
redress of their grievances,

A SERMON

WILL BE PREACHED,

On Sunday next, March 13th. 1825,

AT SIX O' CLOCK IN THE EVENING,

AT THE

WESLEYAN CHAPEL,

DAVENTRY,

BY THE

REV. T. H WALKER,

And a collection made, with the view of relieving such Families in the trade,
in the town of Daventry, as may be judged most necessitous.

The Collection to be at the disposal of a Committee, appointed for that purpose.

Tomalin, Printer, Daventry.

71   Handbill about a footware trade dispute, 1825.

Dissenters in their place. The Industrial Revolution happened somewhere else.

This did not stop Daventry becoming one
of Northamptonshire's footware towns. By 1851
it had nine employers putting out work to 673
workers (including 269 women) in Daventry,
and to others in villages around. In the course
of the next 20 years the number of shoemakers
in the town grew to a peak of around 800,
whilst the number of manufacturers dropped to
five. According to one source, in 1886 Daventry
was producing 450,000 pairs of boots and shoes
and closed-uppers a year, and paying wages to
7-800 workers of about £27,000. The most
successful and longest-lasting was the Leeds and
Leicester firm of Stead & Simpson, which set
up a branch in Daventry in 1844. They came
to employ rather more than half its boot and
shoe workers, and by 1879 had a branch at
Braunstone. Daventry's other principal firm was
of more local origin. Founded by John Marriot
Rodhouse in 1837, it was carried on by his
sons after his death. Rodhouse, in common with
most of the footware manufacturers, was a
Dissenter and an ardent Liberal politician. For

most of his life he and his kind were kept out
of the Moot Hall.[1]

The footware trade was important to
Daventry. Without it, the town's decline would
have been more marked. Overall, it compensated
for the loss of wayfaring business. Its fastest period
of growth was the 1840s when the number of
workers grew from 400 to 700. But after the
1870s it stopped growing as an employer of labour.
It was an industry to which technology came
late, and Daventry was not the sort of place to
attract the capital needed to set up machinery
and build factories. By 1914 the trade was in the
hands of only three firms, Stead & Simpson,
Charles Rodhouse & Son and F.W. Mountain
(later Mountain & Daniel), who by then were
employing around 600 workers. For much of the
Victorian period it was a trade of small employers, a number of whom ended in bankruptcy,
and of workers who were in the main handsewn
men. Riveted boots made their appearance in the
1860s, as did machine sewing (which became
women's work), though neither gave Daventry
much of a boost. Moreover, footware's hand-
craft mode of production failed to stimulate the
formation of other industries found in footware
towns, such as small-scale engineering.

With the growth of footware, the working
classes made their appearance on the scene.
Daventry's workers shared many characteristics
with their artisan forebears, particularly in the
way they worked at home or in small workshops,
but in the early Victorian years some embraced
trade unionism and Radical politics in the form
of Chartism. Daventry's élite regarded shoemakers with even more disdain than their employers,
and the appearance of disputes and strikes in 1825,
1831, 1834 and 1853-4, and the advocacy of
democracy, in the form of the six points of the
People's Charter, aroused fear and hostility and
confirmed them in their prejudices.[2] In the event,
trade unionism, never strong among outworkers,
faded away until the factory era of the late 1880s,
and Chartism was effectively ended by 1850. Later
working-class organisations such as friendly societies, co-operative stores and working men's clubs,
all of which appeared in Daventry in due course,
alarmed them less.

Daventry's market and fairs were harmed,
though not ruined, by the coming of the railway.
A rivalry grew up with Rugby, whose corn and
cheese markets were now in competition with

Daventry's, and the development of Rugby as a railway centre gave Daventry a vision of what-might-have-been. In the 1840s Daventry made efforts to attract the people to the October fairs, with ox-roasts, side-shows and sporting events with attractive prizes.[3] These met with some success. In the period of 'High Farming' in 1856 the fairs were increased from 13 to 14, and in 1868, as a result of a petition from farmers and graziers who argued that 'a uniform day is being adopted in most towns with success', the fairs in Daventry were fixed for the second Tuesday in every month.[5] Yet, if in general local farmers stayed loyal, the failure of Daventry in the 1850s to erect a market house or corn exchange for their convenience, which virtually every other market town did, is indicative of its essential stagnation and lack of enterprise.

Some evidence of Daventry's continuing viability as a market town is shown in the pattern of carriers' routes. In the 18th century there were only one or two Daventry carriers and they conveyed produce people and produce to and from London. By 1824 there were seven, carrying to Birmingham and Northampton as well as the capital. Six years later a considerable change had come over this pattern. Whilst there were still wagons running to and from these places (and Warwick and Banbury as well) a regular weekly service to some 32 villages, nearly all within a radius of eight miles or so, had developed. By then there were no less than 53 carriers operating from Daventry. By 1847 there were 63, going to 40 different destinations.[4] With the coming of the railway they no longer carried to London and Birmingham, though they still did to Coventry and Northampton, Warwick and Banbury. With the growing sophistication of business and the general growth of the economy, the country carrier, linking villages with their market towns and the manufacturing centres beyond, was a familiar figure on the country roads of Victorian England, especially in areas such as Northamptonshire, where cross-country railway lines were not built until later in the century.

Politics

Once the Whig Lord Althorp succeeded to the Spencer earldom in 1834 and his seat in Parliament was taken by Sir Charles Knightley, the recovery of Toryism in South Northamptonshire from the shocks of reform seemed complete. Until 1881

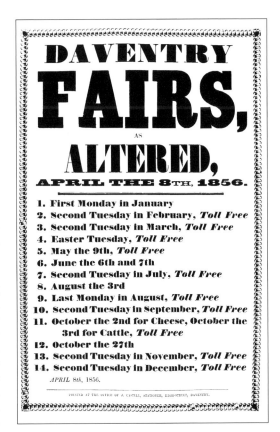

72   Handbill with dates of fairs, 1856.

the two seats went to Conservatives, usually Knightleys and Cartwrights, the only Liberal win being in 1857 when another Lord Althorp intervened. The following year he, like his predecessor, had to resign on becoming a peer, and was succeeded by Col. Henry Cartwright. In 1885, following the Reform Act, the Southern Division became a single-member constituency. Sir Rainald Knightley, MP since 1852, distinctly uncomfortable now that the labourers had the vote, was re-elected, but retired in 1892, after 40 years at Westminster. Conservatives were dismayed by a Liberal victory that year, but won the seat at all subsequent elections (except in 1906) down to the coming of the Great War.

If Daventry's hinterland was unpromising for Whigs and Liberals so was Daventry itself. This only meant they tried that much harder but, unless a Spencer threw his hat into the ring, they were always outnumbered, always outgunned. James Hawker, born in 1836, a shoemaker at the age of

12, remembered Daventry election battles in his childhood: 'When it was a Close-Run I have seen Captain Watkins of Daventry hold up a Ten Pound Note for a Tory vote' [this was probably in 1857].

> They would Engage all the Roughs as Special Constables, not to Keep the Peace but because they might break it. I was one several times. We was marched into the National School and Kept there till the Election was over. There was plenty of Eating and Drinking and five shillings each. They knew if we was at Liberty what Part we should Play. For it was our Natural Instinct to look upon the Tory as our Greatest Enemy.[5]

The Tories also knew how to handle their middle-class opponents in municipal elections, achieving a monopoly on the council for 30 years after the Municipal Reform Act. In the 1840s Liberalism was given a temporary boost by the activities of the Anti-Corn Law League, the occasional battle over church-rate and the odd success in vestry elections or those for guardians of the poor, but the attempts of Dissenters and shoe manufacturers to win seats on the council were usually defeated. The tide began to turn in the early 1860s with the revival of Reform nationally. These years also saw the appearance of the first weekly Daventry newspapers, the Liberal *Spectator* and the Conservative *Express*. In November 1865 four shoe manufacturers were elected to the Council, one of whom was J.M. Rodhouse. Alas for him, he died the following year, at 57. But the breakthrough had been made.

73   The borough seal as used in Daventry borough letterheads in the 1940s.

Two years later the Liberals got a majority on the council. They lost it again in 1873, but regained it in 1879, when Charles Rodhouse, the son of J.M. Rodhouse, became Daventry's mayor.[6] However, despite a persistent Liberal presence from that time on, it was not until 1914 that another Liberal occupied the mayoral chair. In 1873-4 the economic background of the four aldermen and 12 councillors was that two were professional men (a surgeon and a barrister), three were farmers plus a fourth who was an auctioneer and farmer, seven were shopkeepers, whilst shoe manufacturer representation had been reduced to one, in the person of William Line. The political balance then stood at nine Conservatives, six Liberals and one 'neutral'.[7] What is striking about the political scene is how personal and rancorous it was. With such a small number of voters (the Burgess List in 1860 numbered only 513) perhaps this was inevitable.

In 1889, with the first ever election of County councillors, another avenue opened to those with political ambitions. The Conservative expected to contest the seat was E.S. Burton's son, Edmund Charles Burton, but he felt compelled to withdraw because of popular hostility towards him over a libel case he had recently brought. To great Liberal satisfaction Charles Rodhouse was elected (though Burton ousted him next time round). That election also sent another Daventry Liberal to County Hall, E.F. Ashworth Briggs, a barrister. The son of a prominent Daventry citizen, and a descendant of Dr. Ashworth, the principal of the Dissenting Academy a century before, he was a very active Congregationalist. He had been elected to the town council in 1879 and had been suggested as prospective opponent of Sir Rainald Knightley in 1885. However, he set his sights on the County Council and went down to Middleton Cheney and defeated Aubrey T. Cartwright, in a district where the latter's family influence was believed to be paramount. His death, at 36, in a railway accident the following year was a tremendous shock. Daventry Liberalism lost a leader with what everyone assumed was a distinguished political future.[8]

Local government

In the 1860s the Liberals claimed that over the past 30 years Daventry's local government had been lifeless. Because the rate-yield in such a small place was low and because councillors were now answerable to the ratepayers in a way they had not been before 1835, in its early years the council spent very little beyond paying salaries. The problem was that expectations of local government were rising inexorably. The instinct of the council was to try to ignore these as long as possible.

However, it soon became apparent that the old policing arrangements were out of date. In 1839 Northamptonshire adopted the Rural Police Act, and uniformed policemen made their first appearance in the area around. Daventry ratepayers were opposed to the cost of full-time paid police in the borough and it was not until 1857 that two officers were appointed, one of whom was to be head constable, whilst the other was also to be sanitary inspector and inspector of common lodging houses. Daventry's police force remained at that level for the rest of the century, though the force for the Daventry division of the county (34 parishes) came to consist of one superintendent, one inspector, two sergeants and eight constables, for whom a new station house in New Street was erected in 1860. By modern standards there was little crime. In 1889 convictions for indictable offences were nine, against 33 in 1888; drunkenness remained the same at three; and assaults on the police were nil.[9] Daventry's policemen were chiefly occupied in stopping urchins playing in the streets and moving on idlers and undesirables. The appearance of regular policing removed the need for the Daventry Town Association for the Prosecution of Crimes. That did not mean it was wound up. On the contrary, it continued to have its annual meeting each year, an excuse for members to enjoy a convivial evening together at one of Daventry's leading hostelries.

As in other towns, services which would later become part of local government responsibilities were at that time left to private enterprise. The formation of the Gas Company has already been noted. In 1835 the waterworks supplying water from Borough Hill was advertised for sale by the lord of the manor, after the bankruptcy of the last leaseholder. The following year a company was established for the better supplying of the town with soft water, proposing to raise £1,500 in £10 shares.[10] Until the era of improved sanitation 50 years later, Daventry got its water from this source, or in the time-honoured manner from the old wells and pumps in the town.

74 Before policing: Daventry Town Association poster, 1852.

75 Later Victorian Borough letterhead. The Dane is now in classical armour and helmet.

Under the 1806 Act, the responsibility for paving, draining, lighting and sewering lay with the Improvement Commissioners, and they fulfilled these responsibilities in a piecemeal sort of way, concentrating on street improvement. Daventry decided against adopting the first

76   Roasting an ox in celebration of Queen Victoria's Diamond Jubilee in 1897.

(permissive) Public Health Act in 1848 because, if it had done, all the land in the parish would have had to pay one fourth of a rate, which the farmers on the council objected to, and the borough declined to take on this burden. By the 1860s sanitary issues had come to the forefront in Daventry as elsewhere, and discussions between the town council and the commissioners on the sewage problem were at times acrimonious.[11]

In the end the Public Health Act of 1872 forced local authorities, both urban and rural, to face up to their sanitary responsibilities. An inspector of nuisances and a medical officer of health were appointed, and the responsibilities of the Improvement Commissioners devolved to a sanitary committee of the council. The following year a first sewering project was started. Where a borough was not under the Health of Towns Act the charges could be taken out of the borough rate, which raised the question of the exemption of the rural part of the parish. Under the Sanitary Law Amendment Act of 1874 liability for payment of rates was extended to the farms and lands of

the parish. Improving the health of towns in this part of the 19th century was like peeling an onion. The removal of one layer revealed yet another inside it, and yet another. Putting in main sewers led to the problem of sewage disposal, which led to the problem of the disposal of night soil and ashes from the town middens, which led to the problem of an improved water supply, and so on. All improvements were expensive, and ratepayers, especially in very small towns, were obstructive. This in turn led to pressure from the Local Government Board in London, and from 1889 the County Surveyor, to do something about the problems revealed in the annual reports of the medical officer.[12]

That year the medical officer, Dr. Churchouse of Long Buckby, wrote,

> I very much regret that again this year I have nothing on which I can congratulate your authority, the drainage of your town is simply disgraceful, the well-water dangerous to drink from its pollution with sewage matter, the town has not been free from scarlet fever for

77   Celebration dinner in the market place, the Queen's Jubilee, 1897.

more than a week or two at a time during the year, and altogether the sanitary condition of the town is as bad as it can be.[13]

Faced with such pressures and aided by government loans, 'municipal socialism' made its first tentative appearance in Daventry. Over the next decade or so the town built a sewage works, and the council acquired the waterworks company and proceeded to improve the town's water supply by closing the polluted wells and erecting a new reservoir on Borough Hill.

In the later Victorian years two local government issues came to the fore illustrative of the nature of public life in such a small place as Daventry. In both of them the Burton family were prominent. The first was the Moot Hall

affair. As already noted, in 1806 the old Moot Hall had been purchased and demolished and a house in the Hog Market acquired and brought into use as the new Moot Hall. The problem was paying for all this. The old Moot Hall cost £900, the new one £808 and the Act of Parliament sanctioning them £544. Compared with the scale of the corporation's normal financial operations these were enormous sums. In order to raise the money, arrangements were entered into which, in the course of time, became so tangled that a special committee had to be appointed in 1879 to try to sort out the matter. It did not prove easy.

The Act gave the corporation two ways of raising the money. The first was to raise up to

78 A relaxed Daventry *en fête* for the Queen's Jubilee, 1897.

£3,000 in £50 shares from amongst themselves and other subscribers. To ensure a return for the shareholders the stallage on the site of the old Moot Hall was to be let, and so was the new Moot Hall, subject to the right of the corporation to hold their meetings in the building. Their second source of finance available to the corporation was monies vested in it, held in the form of consols and stock. In 1806 these were sold, raising £1,348, of which £537 belonged to the corporation as trustees for certain town charities. This sum, together with 37 shares called up for £20 each, and some sundry subscriptions received by the Bailiff, was used to pay for the purchase of the old and new Moot Halls. From the start, how the Moot Hall finances were managed was unclear. In the words of the committee of inquiry 'both the Bailiff and burgesses, and the shareholders appear to have acted in the management of the undertaking; but it is difficult to define the exact part which each of them took in the matter'. In time the matter became even

more complicated. Tangled up in the arrangements was charity money. Under the Municipal Corporations Act, after 1836 the council ceased to be trustees of the charities and the annual payment of interest to the charities had to be separated from the interest payable on the other part of the corporation stock on loan to the Moot Hall committee.

The situation was further complicated over the letting of the Moot Hall. From 1822 the lessee was Edmund Singer Burton, the town clerk, who used the Moot Hall as his firm's offices and, for a time, his home. In addition to investing money in the project, he, during his lifetime, bought up most of the subscribed shares. After his death in 1863, his executors completed the process by purchasing the rest. The upshot was, by 1869, it was not clear who actually owned the Moot Hall. In 1885 the council was further shaken by the intention of the Attorney General to bring an action against the council for the recovery of £537 plus interest claimed by the trustees of the town charities. The opinion of counsel was sought and he thought it was a case of a trustee mixing trust funds with his own money. When it became clear that the Attorney General was proposing to cause the Moot Hall to be sold to realise the £537 plus interest the ratepayers had to foot the bill. There was an immense row.[14]

The second was the battle over the recreation ground. In 1887 Daventry, along with every other place in the kingdom, debated how it would mark Queen Victoria's golden jubilee. The most popular suggestion was purchasing part of the Inlands to provide the town with a much-needed recreation ground, the cost of which would be £800. Alarmed by this sum, the council threw out this idea and decided instead on a clock for the Moot Hall. However, the supporters of the recreation ground formed a committee and began to try to raise the money. Annoyed by this populist challenge, the council and its advisers raised objections to the Inlands scheme, and in the process, E.C. Burton, the clerk to the Justices and former town clerk, became bitterly unpopular. A sensation was caused when he received a parcel containing the tails of two dead foxes, and notes were sent to him and another member of the Pytchley Hunt to the effect that if they continued to oppose the recreation of the people, and failed to contribute toward the purchase of the recreation ground, the recreation of the hunting fraternity would be interrupted by further acts of vulpicide. It transpired that the sender was a well-to-do Daventry surgeon, Cuthbert Johnson. In November 1888 Burton brought legal actions against Johnson for demanding money with menaces and libel. Johnson admitted to his foolishness in becoming involved in the matter and was found not guilty on the first count, but was sentenced to a month in prison on the second. Amongst the populace his prosecution was seen as persecution. Burton became even more unpopular. When Johnson was released from prison he was met at the station by a large crowd who gave him a hero's welcome. The horses were unhitched from his carriage, and he was pulled home by the crowd, to the accompaniment of the Daventry Working Men's band playing 'A Soldier and a Man'. It was this which led Burton to withdraw from the first County Council election. The upshot was that, with the help of a committee of working men, the rest of the money was quickly raised, the land purchased

79   The top end of High Street after 1911, when the Burton Memorial was erected. Behind (*right*) is the Moot Hall.

and in 1890 the Jubilee Recreation ground, whose management was vested in a committee of 17, subject to control by the Charity Commissioners, was officially opened by the Mayor. Dr. Johnson, who had since left the town, was there and received a hearty cheer. Mr. Burton was not. Eventually the ownership of the recreation ground was vested in the council.

Burton died in 1907. Four years later, a memorial in the form of a cross in the decorated Gothic style of architecture, standing 39 feet high, was erected. The niche on the west side of the central shaft contained a drinking fountain above which a bronze plate (now missing) had the following words: 'To the Memory of Edmund Charles Burton, MA, Of The Lodge, Daventry. Born September 4th, 1826, died August 20th, 1907. Educated at Westminster School, and Christ Church, Oxford'. The plate in the north niche has this inscription:

This Memorial was placed here in remembrance of Edmund Charles Burton by members past and present of the National

Hunt Committee, his personal friends, and others who esteemed him. A staunch Churchman, a renowned sportsman, and a man greatly beloved. By his life he set an example of what a true English gentleman should be, and whether in sport, business, or pleasure, it can be truly said of him 'sans peur et sans reproch'.

If that was how the friends of Burton wanted him remembered, it was also a message that in the battle over the recreation ground the foxhunting fraternity were determined to have the last word.[15]

Religion and education

For the rest of the century the pattern established by 1840 of two places of worship belonging to the established Church, one Congregationalist and one Wesleyan chapel remained unchanged. The only addition was the re-appearance of Catholicism in 1882, after an absence of three centuries, with the mission church of St Mark in London Road. The number of Catholics, however, remained small. In the case of the Church, the battle to improve the value of the living was finally won in the time of Canon Collyns, who persuaded Christ Church to restore the great tithes and make the living into a rectory. Eventually Christ Church exchanged the advowson for that of another living and the right of presentation passed into the hands of the Bishop of Peterborough. In 1874 Holy Cross was re-seated and in 1884 given a major redecoration.[16] As in other towns, religious division, with the Church remaining the dominant force, continued to be the basis of many of the institutions and the politics of the town into the 20th century, particularly in the case of education.

The disgraceful

saga of the Free Grammar School continued. In 1820, towards the end of the long tenure of the Rev. William Fallowfield as master, the town clerk, writing to the Charity Commisssioners, observed 'at present there are not more than eight or ten boys whose parents choose to send them to the school'. For much of the rest of the century it continued to present the spectacle of a failing school. After Fallowfield there was the Rev. Thomas Sanders, who departed for Moulton vicarage in 1838, though he remained master until 1857. By then the school had dwindled to almost nothing, and the schoolhouse was unfit for use. A new master, the Rev. G.J. Corser, curate of Norton, was appointed and funds were raised to restore the building, which carries a crumbling plaque inscribed 'Restavrata 1857'. Corser employed an assistant to help him teach classics and mathematics and took in boarders. After him, however, the school declined again. In 1871 the mayor wrote to the Charity Commissioners to say that it was too old fashioned and had ceased to be attended by any pupils except that one obstinate burgess insisted on sending his son to learn Latin free. Two years later it was closed.[17] It was reopened as the Endowed Grammar School by the Rev. C.F. Hutton, who was appointed in 1882. It moved to North Street where new buildings were opened, including Warden's lodge, a house for the headmaster. With the coming of the railway, Hutton thought he saw an opportunity for a boarding school for girls, with only a limited number of day pupils. The master who finally made the school viable was the Rev. H.M. Logan. When he arrived in 1891 there were only six boarders, but he soon had 28, making 69 boys in all. The following year there were 80. The school now taught mathematics, the classics and 'the

80 Daventry Grammar School badge, about 1890.

ordinary subjects taught in school' and the master had plans for the introduction of technical education and a chemistry laboratory. The girls' school existed alongside it.[18]

What really made a difference to education was the 1902 Education Act, which brought local education authorities into being. By 1914 the school had become a mixed secondary school under the County Education Committee. It continued to take boarders, and the mistresses and girl boarders resided in a house in Sheaf Street. With regard to the other schools in the town, in 1870 the British School in Foundry Place was re-built and enlarged. It was enlarged again in 1895 and by then had places for 242 children, and its master, Frederick Billingham, sat on the town council as a Liberal. It was eventually merged with a new elementary school opened by the Local Education Authority in St James Street. By 1914 the main school in the town, the English Charity and National School, had come under its aegis and moved into a new building on the site of the old abbey house, becoming generally referred to as the Abbey School. In 1859 a school for 45 children (mixed infants) was built in Drayton and endowed with eight shares in the Daventry Gas Company.[19] It was still there in 1910. Down to about 1906 there was no thought that Daventry elementary schools would send many pupils to the Grammar School, which drew many of its students from outside the town. Elementary education was for working-class children; secondary education was for those whose parents could pay for it. Even when scholarships became available very few Daventry children who passed them took them up. This did not change until after the Second World War.

Associational life

Daventry may have had an undynamic economy, but that did not prevent it developing the network of voluntary associations found in most Victorian towns. By 1855 there were seven registered friendly societies.[20] Banded together on a voluntary basis to insure themselves and their families in time of sickness and against the costs of funerals, they represented the Victorian spirit of self-help. The oldest was the Daventry Friendly Society, founded in 1794. The next oldest were the Original Union Benefit Society and the Daventry Church Union Benefit Society of Tradesmen, founded in 1808 and 1814

respectively. The coming of the workhouse era brought the 'Friend In Need' Benefit Society, the 'Centre of England' Lodge of the Manchester Unity of Odd Fellows, the 'Imperial Crown Lodge' and the 'Widow and Orphans Protection Lodge' of the Nottingham Ancient Imperial Order of Odd Fellows, and Tent 'United Brothers', Independent Order of Rechabites, the temperance friendly society. Soon they were joined by a Court ('Old Dane Tree') of the Ancient Order of Foresters and a branch of the Ancient Order of Shepherds. The latter, like the Odd Fellows, belonged to national 'affiliated orders' with branches all over the country and in some countries abroad.

Convivial clubs as well as insurance bodies, friendly societies contributed to the public life of the town. Celebrating its Jubilee in 1854, members of the Church Union Benefit Society processed to church 'headed by an elegant new flag, raised by subscription, and painted by Mr. S. Cox', where they received a 'forcible and appropriate sermon' from the Rev. D. Veysie, after which more than a hundred sat down to the dinner at the *Fox and Hounds*. The vicar, supported by his senior and junior curates, presided over the after-dinner entertainments and the following day saw the annual tea party and ball for the benefit of the widows and orphans connected with the Society. Aware of the strength of their numbers, in the later Victorian years the Odd Fellows and Foresters organised 'amalgamated demonstrations' to raise money for good causes: in 1891 they got together to start an annual sports day on Whit Monday.[21]

Co-operation came to Daventry in 1859 when a group of working men started a store, with capital raised among themselves. As with all such ventures, progress was steady rather than spectacular until the 1890s, when membership accelerated. By 1900 the Daventry Society had 708 members, a large store in High Street, a branch at Braunston, a 13-acre estate in Daventry (West Lodge) and had built a terrace of cottages. The Daventry Working Men's Club started in 1877. By 1892 it had a membership of 120.[22] Trades unionism, long dormant in Daventry, revived in 1889 with the formation of a branch of the National Union of Boot and Shoe Operatives. Within two years it had 300 members and had negotiated wage statements with the employers. Mindful of the growth of Labour, a letter in the newspaper in 1892 called for co-operators, and friendly society and trade union members to get themselves organised to elect some of their leading men on to the town council, though in fact it was some time before they did.[23]

The middle classes did not need friendly societies to provide them with social security, but they had their organisations too. In 1860, in the wave of patriotism aroused by the threat of war with France, Daventry formed its own Company of Rifle Volunteers. Having to provide their own uniforms, though the government supplied the rifles, it was necessarily an association of the better-off (boot and shoe workers joined the Militia, the older Reserve force). The Volunteers met regularly for drill and rifle practice, the highlight of their year being the annual camp and review with the other Northamptonshire Rifle Companies at such venues as Althorp Park or Norton Park. The aristocracy and gentry gave the movement their strong support, Captain the 5th Earl Spencer being a notable Rifle Volunteer himself. At the company level members revelled in the military rank Volunteering gave them, Daventry's leading figure being E.C. Burton. When the Volunteers became the Volunteer Battalion of the Northamptonshire Regiment as a result of Cardwell's army reforms, he became Major E.C. Burton, Commandant, L Company. Another middle-class association which took root in Daventry was freemasonry. 'Beneventa' Lodge was opened in 1891, its lodge room being at the *Wheat Sheaf*.[24]

Another characteristic organisation, one with a mission to 'reform' the working-class, was the Temperance Association. As a result of the efforts of the South Midlands Temperance Association, a Total Abstinence Society was founded in 1837, and a Temperance Coffee House and reading room was opened in Warwick Road. As a small town with relatively few chapel-goers and many public houses Daventry was never one of Temperance's strongholds. The memories of William Webb ('An old Native Resident') of life in Early Victorian Daventry printed in the newspaper in 1908 underline the problem:

> Drinking with all its attendant evils ran riot, often extending over three days; Saint Monday was faithfully kept and scarcely a Saturday night passed without street fighting unmolested by the parish constable … dog-fighting, cock-fighting, and badger baiting, sometimes on Sunday, all generously patronised by all classes alike, many of whom were professional poachers.[25]

81   Daventry Rifle Volunteers, *c.*1870.

Sport and pastimes

In time newer forms of pastimes arrived in Daventry, as elsewhere. Cricket became the first of the new team games to become popular. In 1858 there are accounts of matches between Daventry and Brington and Daventry Artisans and Northampton Amateurs. As with many sports, cricket was taken up first by the middle class but soon spread more widely. Works teams were got up for matches. In 1877 a party from Stead & Simpson's factory in Leicester arrived to play a match against the Daventry branch. Cycling appeared in 1875 when, watched by a large crowd, the first of a series of monthly races for the captainship, from Daventry to Staverton and back (4 miles), was won by Mr. J. Edward Rodhouse in 16 minutes.[26] The first cyclists were middle-class but, despite the cost of the machines, it soon attracted working men, none of whom was keener than James Hawker, though he did his cycling after he had left Daventry for Northampton. Daventry Football Club was in being by 1890 (with a muscular christian, the Rev. Harold W. Johnson BA., as its hon. secretary). Set in one of the most famous of England's hunting countries, the pleasures of riding featured in Victorian Daventry's pastimes. As well as the meets of the Pytchley, a Daventry steeplechase event was organised in 1838, but it was not until the 1870s that regular meetings were established, though they do not seem to have gone on much after 1877. But in 1883 a regular Foal and Yearling Show was established which soon became the Daventry and District Horse Show and was an annual event down to the Great War.[27]

For those with gentler interests, Daventry offered a number of opportunities and events. The Daventry Horticulture and Floral Society, started in 1835, was still going strong 38 years later. With that delicate social gradation beloved of such bodies, prizes in 1873 were offered in three classes: gentlemen and gardeners (ie. gentlemen's gardeners), amateurs, and cottagers. In the 1850s there was an annual Gooseberry and Currant show, and the Working Men's Club started annual Flower and Vegetable and Chrysanthemum shows in the 1880s. The year 1893 saw the formation of the Dane Tree Fanciers Society for 'promoting the growth, multiplication and improvement of

82 Early Temperance poster, 1842. Mr. T. Cook, of Leicester, was the founder of the firm of Thomas Cook & Son, which started the modern excursion business.

rabbits, poultry, pigeons and cage birds'.[28] As already noted, the holding of balls, dances, assemblies and concerts remained popular into the later 19th century, and in 1871 a new Assembly Hall was opened off New Street, which became the usual venue for these and a wide range of other events, and was used by the Volunteers as its drill hall.

In all these activities Daventry was a microcosm of Victorian urban life, a place where people were just as capable of making as much of their daily lives as elsewhere. There is, however, no denying its continuing economic decline, a decline added to by the Agricultural Depression, which began to take effect in 1879 and lasted down to the Great War.

Nine

The Long Decline Continued: Daventry 1914 to 1945

In some ways Daventry was not unprepared for the First World War. In 1913 there were large-scale military exercises in Northamptonshire, the like of which had not been seen before, and for 30 years the Volunteers and the Yeomanry Reserve Forces had drilled and trained for war. In 1914 they were mobilised and went off to fight with the Northamptonshire Regiment. Daventry, too, played its part in the amazing outburst of volunteering with which the country's young men responded to Kitchener's call for new armies to fight the Germans. But none could have foreseen the length and scale of the war, the immense losses and the terrible testing it gave the nation's reserves of fortitude. Everywhere the mounting death toll caused immense distress in local communities. Whether or not this was worse in small places than in the big industrial cities is not certain, but it must have been acute in a towns as small as Daventry, where everyone knew everyone else with a particular familiarity.

Not all the effects of the war were negative. Government orders placed with businessmen, particularly with those in footware, brought big profits and full employment. Agriculture, for so long in the doldrums, reverted once more to its old role of being the provider of the nation's food, though farmers had to suffer government direction, as did the railways and the coalmines. Women were widely used in what had always

83   The motor car era. Daventry Bowling Club off to Builth Wells, 1922.

been men's jobs, and the war, as all modern wars do, accelerated social change, though probably less in Daventry than in bigger places. The strain of war came to a climax in early 1918 with the German breakthrough on the Western front. After four years of trench warfare the war became one of movement. The German advance was stopped and then massively reversed. By November the Germans sued for peace and it ended with an armistice. The national sense of relief was immense. What followed was a desire to commemorate the dead. On Daventry's war memorial are the names of 114 dead or missing in action, a sizeable proportion of their age group. No one doubted the human cost, but what was not so immediately apparent was the destruction of Britain's international trading network, the basis of its industrial wealth. The country would never be able to reconstruct it.

By the end of the Great War the motor car era had arrived. With the revival of roads as main lines of national communication, long-distance traffic once more passed through Daventry along London Road and Sheaf Street. It was not long before the narrowness of the latter began to cause congestion and hold-ups. This remained so until 1928 when a Ministry of Transport sponsored scheme led to the construction of Western Way, Daventry's first by-pass which, as its name explained, took traffic round the town on the west. The revival of the national road system did not have such beneficial effects on Daventry's economy in the 20th century as in the past. It brought some business to its hotels and public houses, though nothing like that in the days of the stagecoaches, and the by-pass diverted people away from rather than in to the town. Cycle shops, garages and small businesses connected with transport and road haulage were established, but none were great employers of labour. Daventry's communications were improved by the introduction of bus services. By 1928 there was a daily bus to Northampton, one to Leamington on Wednesdays, Saturdays and Sundays, one to Banbury on Thursday and one to Rugby on a Monday.[1] But the major new industries of motor-car manufacturing never came nearer than Coventry, nor electrical engineering nearer than Rugby. Down to the end of the Second World War Daventry's staple industry remained footware. But there was now only firm, Stead & Simpson, whose workforce remained around 500 people.

If that business had flourished in the War, it did less well in the 1920s and '30s.

The modern world impacted on Daventry, and Daventry impacted on the modern world from 1925, the year the new British Broadcasting Company chose Borough Hill as the location for its 21st transmitting Station, '5XX'. Daventry was chosen as a place of maximum contact with the landmass of England and Wales, a radius of 100 miles drawn round it touching the sea at only three points. Shortly before 7.30p.m. on 27 July, John Reith, the managing director of the Company, spoke the words 'Daventry Calling', briefly introduced the new station to the unseen audience, and then (a typical Reithian touch) read the poem *Dane-Tree*, specially written for the occasion by Alfred Noyes. Noyes had brushed up on Borough Hill's history, no doubt in William Edgar's *Borough Hill (Daventry), And its History*, published only two years before, though what really appealed to the poet were stories of the burial of the slain in a great battle on the hill between Mercians and Danes, and the old Dane Tree:

> Daventry calling ... Dark and still,
> The dead men sleep, at the foot of the hill.
> The dark tree, set on the height by the Dane
> Stands like a sentry over the slain

After this, the 2L0 Military Band opened the programme with Elgar's 'Pomp and Circumstance'.[2]

A large proportion of the population of the country was within crystal range of Daventry. Its reception area spread as far as Manchester in the north, London in the south-east and Cardiff in the west. The sale of crystal sets increased enormously. For a while Daventry basked in the fame of being 'the world's biggest broadcasting station'. The coming of the BBC brought local benefits. In the inter-war years a third of Daventry's rate-income came from the Corporation, technical staff came to live in the area and some new jobs were created for local people, though not many. The coming of the BBC also introduced electricity into the town, supplied from Northampton.

Daventry and the BBC had a 67-year relationship. In that time there were many developments in the Corporation's use of Borough Hill. In 1932 the new Empire Service was broadcast from Daventry on short-wave transmission, and two years later all Daventry's long-wave broadcasting was transferred to Droitwich, better placed to improve coverage of the north-west, the south-west and

84 The official party at the opening of Daventry Wireless Station in 1925. In the centre is Sir William Mitchell-Thomson, Bart., Postmaster-General in the Baldwin government. On his right is Councillor I.H. Johnson, Mayor of Daventry, and behind them, John (later Lord) Reith, the presiding genius of the BBC in its formative years.

85 Radio masts on Borough Hill, about 1940.

central development area, 43 acres of land between the old railway and the A45 trunk road were to be a second housing estate, Inlands. South of that, the 93 acres of Stefan Hill were to become Daventry's third housing estate, which was continued westwards as the Grange estate (another 114 acres of housing). North of the Grange was more housing, on 38 acres round Drayton village, and a sixth development was a private one on 51 acres completing the Headlands estate. The second of Daventry's industrial districts, Royal Oak, was laid out to the north-west of all this, abutting the site of Daventry's first major green-field industrial development, that of the British Timken factory. Finally, the plan envisaged two future North Development areas, one south of Drayton Reservoir for housing, and one for industrial purposes, to be located west of the road to Welton. In addition to all this space for housing and the location of new industry, there was to be massive investment in new roads, schools, colleges and shopping centres. Open spaces were provided, one of which became a country park, and plans were made for shopping developments in old Daventry town centre.

In the second half of the '60s the project got off to a flying start. Birmingham purchased nearly 1,000 acres of land, almost bringing Daventry's farming history to a close. Contracts were let for system-built homes designed by the Birmingham city architect, J.A. Maudsley. On the Headlands, Southbrook and Grange estates hundreds of new dwellings were speedily erected. By 1972 about a thousand families had moved in from Birmingham, and another 120 from Essex. New firms arrived bringing new jobs. The largest was the Ford Motor Company Spare Parts Depot, employing 1,250 people. It took a quarter of a million square feet on the Royal Oak industrial estate, erecting a warehouse described at the time as 'the largest single storey building in Britain'. The coming of Herbert Ingersoll, an Anglo-American tool manufacturer, who chose Daventry for its central position in the country, was hailed as a portent. Ingersoll soon failed, but its operation was taken over by Cummins Diesel Engine Plant, one of some 35 worldwide, which soon became Daventry's second largest employer: by 1994 its workforce was over 700. Another early firm was Craelius, from Birmingham. By 1976 the Long March Industrial Estate was said to be 'full up', and only 30 acres of the Royal Oak

Estate remained undeveloped. Jobs and homes were linked, and the exodus from Birmingham at first exceeded predictions. On the other hand, the closure of Stead & Simpson in 1972, after more than a century in the town, was a break with the past, though for some years the factory continued to be used for the manufacture of footwear by the firm of White of Earls Barton.

In these years there were changes to the centre of old Daventry.[3] The core of the town behind High Street, Sheaf Street and New Street was demolished and a new shopping precinct with its own parking opened in 1973. In the process, most of the buildings in New Street went, and not long after much of St James Street was demolished. High Street was made a conservation area and the sensitive way in which it was improved and lit attracted praise from architects and town planners. Sheaf Street, on the other hand, was neglected and with each passing year its decay worsened. Moreover, as a result of these developments, the town centre emptied. With new roads around it acting as a *cordon sanitaire*, severing it from the newly built suburbs, it took on a melancholy air.

By 1976 Daventry's population had reached an estimated 15,750. In all its history it had seen nothing like this decade of growth. But by then it was becoming clear, and had been for some time, that expansion was slowing. Indeed, with the virtue of hindsight, it is apparent that its most rapid phase of growth was already over. As early as 1968 the building of houses was outstripping the number of people moving into the town. Daventry was also failing to attract new firms, a process made more difficult in the early 1970s by the refusal of the Board of Trade to grant Industrial Development certificates, preferring to see the re-location of industry to more deprived areas, such as the North East. It seemed a classic case of the right hand of government not knowing what the left was doing, or, more accurately, knowing but being unable to reconcile the two. It created a crisis in Daventry's development. At one point it almost seemed that all those millions invested in the infrastructure of schools, roads, sewers and housing were going to be wasted. Deputations were sent to the Ministry of Housing and Local Government and heated exchanges with more than one Minister and their civil servants resulted. In the end there came a suggestion that experiments should be tried with small factory units (which did not need Industrial Development certificates) and which could be offered on reasonably long leases. The idea was a great success. The units went almost immediately. 'Small is beautiful' turned out to be Daventry's industrial salvation, and was emulated elsewhere.[4] In trying to attract new firms, particularly from the South, Daventry always faced competition from new towns such as Milton Keynes, or places undergoing planned expansion such as Northampton or Wellingborough. Nonetheless, Daventry was able to hold its own. With its favourable central location close to national road and rail routes, it became clear that Daventry's future lay as a warehouse and distribution centre. That is what brought Green Shield and later Argos, Gilbey Vintners and Volvo as well as Ford and Cummins. By the mid-1970s Daventry had a reasonably flourishing industrial sector and a lower rate of unemployment than many other new towns.

By then Daventry's expansion was put on hold, at any rate for the time being, by the government's call in 1975 to local authorities to cut spending. Twelve years of 'stop-go' in the economy had taken its effect. Post-war planning was based on assumptions of annual growth rates in the economy which were, in fact, never achieved. On top of that were the effects of a sharp rise in inflation. Facing 'stagflation', Prime Minister James Callaghan famously remarked that as far as ever- increasing government spending was concerned, 'the party was over'. In Daventry an immediate casualty was the County Council's scheme for a road to open up Dunslade, a third industrial estate.

Another factor made it clear that the first phase in the history of 'new' Daventry was drawing to a close. Birmingham, which had invested £14 million in the project, was developing cold feet. Put simply, Daventry was no longer as important to that city as it once had been. There were several reasons. Birmingham people had always been willing enough to move to Daventry, but the plan to transfer industry had never worked as intended. Whatever the City Council, the Government or the planners had envisaged, entrepreneurs were not minded to relocate. By 1975 the City Council no longer wanted them to anyway. The firms that did come to Daventry came from elsewhere in the Midlands, from the south or from abroad. It had also become apparent that the Birmingham conurbation had more than enough 'overspill towns', and that Daventry was too far away for people to commute comfortably. More importantly, with the inflation of the period pushing up local government borrowing interest rates, the cost to the Birmingham ratepayers was becoming too high. In 1976 Birmingham announced that it was pulling out of the planning partnership. It rapidly became clear that the ambition for Daventry to grow to a population of anything like 36,000 was not going to be realised. Nonetheless what had happened over the past 12 years had been a model exercise in town planning.

To an impressive degree what the Daventry Town Development Committee and its planners set out to do they did. By 1976 seven major housing developments and two industrial estates had been brought into being. If they were not as advanced as was originally planned, all were well on the way to completion. New schools had been built and opened, new shopping facilities had been provided, and the planned road system was well-advanced. A scheme for the conversion of the 130-acre site of the redundant British Waterways Reservoir into a country park had just been put forward, which in the future was to prove a very popular amenity. The relationship between Birmingham, Northamptonshire and Daventry was in many ways an exemplary exercise in local government co-operation. All the parties had fulfilled their obligations efficiently and without rivalry or politicking. If, in the end, Birmingham withdrew, it did so on generous terms, and by then all were aware that the political climate was changing. If the planned population growth target was only half achieved, Daventry was renewed and revitalised, and maybe for a place with a small-town history, a population of 18,000 was more comfortable than one double the size. When the tripartite Development Committee held its final meeting, in 1986, the relationship ended as it had always been conducted, amicably.

In the 12 years of Daventry's expansion there were disappointments for some and setbacks for others. There were always those who regretted the days when Daventry was small, quiet and comfortable, and they hated being force-fed with modernity. Above all they did not like the fact that Daventry was now full of strangers. As usual with new towns, it was to take time for incomers to feel at home on the housing estates or to feel that they really belonged, though their children soon did. There were also examples of the way that growth at the fiat of planners and politicians was rarely trouble-free. Daventry had its white elephants. Notable amongst these was the *John o'Gaunt* Hotel. Built in 1974, with its 100 bedrooms and conference facilities, it was conceived as a major asset. However, beset with constructional problems and owned by a property company that went bankrupt, for four years it stood unused, to some a symbol of how planning could go wrong. Eventually it was opened as the *Penguin Hotel*. Today it is the *Britannia*. On the housing front, system building was not always a success. It was remarkable how quickly some of Daventry's new housing aged. In 1978 the award-winning Grange estate, all of nine years old, was described as looking like a slum. Twelve years later, a Professor from London University, invited to visit Southbrook, then attracting attention for its high crime rate, declared that some of its problems arose from the fact that it had been badly designed and recommended re-planning its community facilities.

Daventry's development under the District Council

The withdrawal of Birmingham coincided with the most important change in the organisation of local government for almost a century. Under the 1972 Local Government Act, Daventry became part of a new and largely rural district authority which stretched away to the east to the edges of Northampton and Market Harborough, much of it well beyond Daventry's traditional market area. The area to the south, physically and historically much closer to Daventry, became part of the new District of South Northamptonshire. Although it gave its name to the new district, with only 20 per cent of the overall population, the town was reduced to relative unimportance. What grieved Daventry patriots more was the end of borough status, after almost four centuries. Past and present members of the borough council took this affront to their history hard. Councillors newly elected for Daventry wards, now in a permanent minority on the District Council, constituted themselves the Daventry Charter Trustees, a sort of government in exile. Since 1974, with all due pomp and ceremony, they have continued to elect a town mayor, a sort of unofficial (and occasionally

embarrassing) rival to the chairman of the District Council. Their stronghold at first was the old Moot Hall, certain rooms of which, containing the relics of the old Borough corporation and council, were denied the District Council. Too small anyway for the new council's needs, temporary new premises close by were occupied. No longer the seat of Daventry's local government, the Moot Hall eventually came into use as an information centre and home to a new museum. To this day the Charter Trustees have never given up the idea that the old borough area might regain some element of self-government. Another organisation founded in the aftermath of re-organisation and the demise of the Borough Council was the Daventry and District Society. Since 1978 it has kept an eye on the many changes proposed to the fabric of the town, fighting for the preservation of what is worth saving of historic Daventry and keeping a vigilant eye open on the likely effects of planning decisions.

After Birmingham's withdrawal the County Council and District Council took over responsibility for Daventry's further development. Birmingham sold the remaining land it held to the District Council on favourable terms, and in 1980 the District Planning Committee produced a revised 10-year Town Plan in accordance with the County Structural Plan.[5] It proposed a revised target population of 24,000 for Daventry by 1991 (an increase of 7,000) and the completion of the development of the original housing estates and road system. The main new proposal was to develop 320 acres or so of the Northern Area. There was to be a new industrial estate, optimistically envisioned to provide around 5,400 jobs, and land was to be earmarked for private housing. A further aim was to rebuild and 'bring back life to the town centre'. In this conservation figured highly, with landscaping, the pedestrianisation of Sheaf Street, and cycleways.

Planners and local councillors may plan, but outcomes are always affected by central government priorities, and all these in turn by the state of the economy generally. At the time of writing (1999) it is 20 years since the government of Mrs. Thatcher came to power, and these two decades constitute a different phase to the one that preceded it. Under her, the era of urban growth through New Towns was speedily brought to a close, though the developments they set in train were not. 'Socialism had failed' and

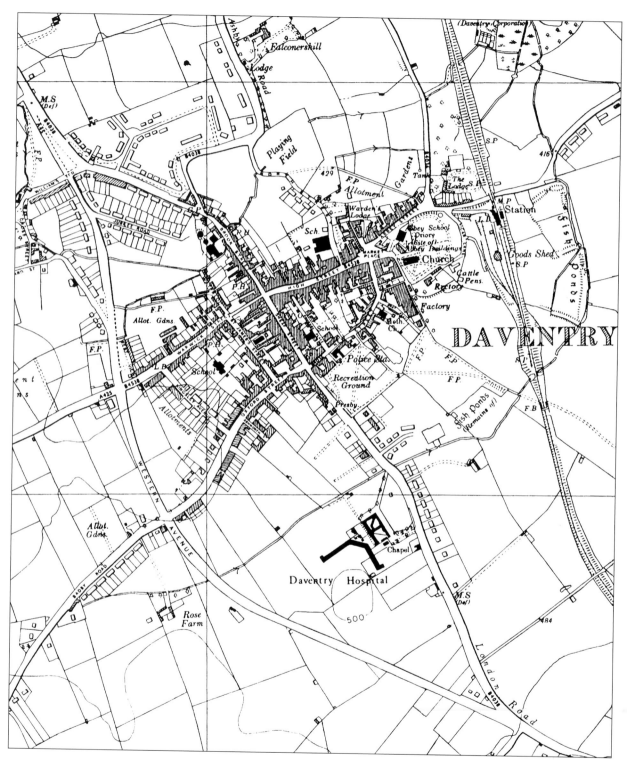

90 Before the great expansion: Daventry in 1958.

91   Air photograph of Daventry's expansion in 1984, taken from the north.

government spending was to be curbed. Victorian values (or what were imagined as Victorian values) were invoked. Social objectives were to be achieved largely through the working of market forces. The very next year, local government spending on housing was cut by two-thirds. In Daventry this meant that the fifth and final stage

in the construction of the Southbrook estate escaped the axe by a whisker, and in future most new housing was to be built and new industrial estates developed by private enterprise, or so it was envisioned. 'Thatcherism', or the beginnings of it, as we have seen, predated Thatcher. However, not even Mrs. Thatcher could make

92   A surveyor at work expanding Daventry. In the background the Herbert-Ingersoll Factory.

the British economy tigerish, though that did not prevent her government claiming that it had.

In fact the two decades since 1979 have been characterised by cycles of depression and boom not dissimilar to those which preceded them (though inflation was brought under control by a government obsessed by it). In Daventry, as elsewhere, the early '80s were dominated by large-scale unemployment (especially among school-leavers) brought on by cuts in public expenditure. In 1981-2 in the town the jobless figure was said to be 'at an all time high'. Then, from mid-decade, there was another period of economic expansion in which Britain was invited to believe that it was 'the fastest growing economy in Europe'. Daventry's local economy recovered and by 1986 the town was said to be experiencing a shortage of skilled labour. Nonetheless, as

measured by population growth over the decade, Daventry's expansion was modest. By the time of the 1991 census it had grown by only 2,000. The following decade this pattern was repeated. Overall, it must be said that Daventry did reasonably well on the economic front. Reviewing national and regional prospects in 1994, a boom year, the economic forecasters of the Henley Centre noted the quality of Daventry's communications, the strengths of its small business networks and the lively state of its property market.

On the industrial front, the optimism behind Daventry's New Town Plan for the vigorous development of the Northern Area was damaged by the recession of the early '80s. At its heart is the story of the attempted development of the Lang Farm estate. Lying outside the original expansion plan for Daventry, this farm was acquired by a private property developer in 1964 and he later acquired a further 50 acres adjoining. In 1972 Lang Farm was added to the Daventry Town Plan, and government approval given for development of both industry and housing. However, fearing competition with its own projects, Daventry Borough Council refused Welton House Estates Ltd. planning permission. In 1980, the government's emphasis on relying on private enterprise, together with the publication of the New Town Plan, gave a new impulse to the idea of Lang Farm's development, and the District Council gave planning approval. The following year consent was also given for the building of one and a quarter miles of new road to link the A361 near Lang Farm to the Southway/Easternway roundabout, the last major link in Daventry's ring road system, held up for economic reasons for five years. However, the private development of Lang Farm was hit by the recession. In three years the company failed to attract any firms to its industrial estate, and in 1983 went into liquidation. Two years later the District Council bought the property. Because the Council had just started to develop its own Industrial Estate at Drayton Fields, at the other end of the new road, it was decided that the future of the land at Daventry Park (as Lang Farm was now called) lay with housing rather than industry. In the '80s Business Parks were a feature of every Planning Department's portfolio, and Daventry launched its own in 1989. It too made an inauspicious start, a victim of the depression of the time: after its first 17 months it had still failed to attract any tenants. However, things began to move on this front when the economy came out of recession. The German firm of Schenk commenced business in Daventry Heartland Park in 1994 and it was announced that Marconi was to open a major experimental centre there. Another Northern Area development which suffered from unlucky timing was the new *Holiday Inn* on the A361, which opened in 1990. Two years later it was bought by Resort Hotels and renamed *Daventry Resort Hotel*.

These 20 years saw important additions to (and subtractions from) to the list of enterprises in Daventry. It was in 1980 that the huge new warehousing of Gilbey Vintners opened on the Royal Oak Estate, and it was soon joined there by the Volvo Training Centre, which was expanded five years later. This development was only part of the growing local presence of this Swedish company: 1981 saw the opening of the Volvo centre at Crick, which, located just off the M1 motorway, developed as a major warehousing centre in the Daventry district. In 1988, Midland Meat Packers Ltd., described as the biggest plant in Britain in that particular business, commenced operations there. By far the most spectacular development at Crick, however, is the Daventry International Rail Freight Terminal, which opened in 1997. On a 350-acre site, four million square feet of manufacturing and distribution buildings, some with their own railway sidings, are being developed, with the promise of 5,000 new jobs. Located next to the electrified West Coast rail line, DIRFT is designed to have a direct link to every major road and rail network in Britain and Europe. But there were casualties on the industrial front. Argos and British Timken in Daventry folded in the depression of the early '90s, the latter a sad loss. Timken had been the catalyst in Daventry's modern development, and for almost four decades one of its major employers. The town had also been a beneficiary of the Nene Foundation, the Timken family charitable trust.

Over these 20 years the same economic and political forces which affected industry and employment determined the development of Daventry's housing sector. As we have seen, the planners' plans of 1980 were halted by government spending cuts, and there followed a three-year property depression. By 1985 demand for housing had recovered. That year saw a further addition to Southbrook of 30 homes, shops and a new church. But the major Daventry housing scene was to be the Northern Area. 1985 also saw the start of the first of four development phases on Daventry Park. Seen as 'a milestone in the development of Daventry', this was a large-scale project envisioning the construction of 2,000 private houses, many to be 'executive homes'. The first was Ashby Fields. There were also to be shops, a public house and a health centre. In 1988 the scheme was revised. Under a 'new revised Northern Area plan' the objective was now to provide 3,000 houses by the year 2001 on Ashby Fields, Lang Farm South, Welton Road and Middlemore.

Further demands for yet more new houses in Daventry soon materialised. Under a new District Plan in 1990 it was proposed that another 1,780 new homes be built in Daventry. A year later the

93 The results of the great expansion: Daventry in 1981.

government, modifying the County Council Structure Plan, added another 500 houses. Two years later (1993) the government increased its demands on the District to provide further homes, 1,071 of which were to be in Daventry. The location of these presented problems to Daventry's planners, now running short of building land. Eventually the proposals were for them to be at Middlemore, Drayton Park and Burnt Walls. The latter, a site of historic and environmental interest, caused controversy, and was turned down. It was replaced by plans to build on the old British Timken site. In spite of these constantly raised targets, the true growth of the town in the first six years of the decade was modest. The official estimate of Daventry's population in 1996 was 19,087, just under a thousand more than in 1991. (The current projected population for the year 2006 is 22,831).

The New Town Plan of 1980 ushered in many changes in the centre of Daventry. The long decay of Sheaf Street was arrested with a pedestrianisation and improvement scheme, though the placing of a gazebo at the top end of its hill never seems less than odd, given that gazebos belong more to country gardens than the middle of town streets. Another severance with the past in that street was the closure of the *Wheat Sheaf* as a public house. It found a new life as a nursing home. The proposal to demolish Daventry's last remaining Victorian terrace in St James Street led to a resistance campaign mounted

by the Daventry and District Society, which eventually met with success in 1983. The public library and the Royal Cinema were both rebuilt. After a fire destroyed their temporary premises, new offices for the District Council were opened in 1987 at a cost of more than £4 million.

The Daventry Town Strategy of 1992, the object of which was to 'give the town centre a facelift' continued the process. The New Street shopping area, now 20 years old, was improved and updated. Plans were also discussed for a new supermarket and a battle began over whether or not out-of-town supermarket sites should be sanctioned. The idea was opposed by those in the centre and by local politicians. But the more supermarkets develop, whether in or out, the more traditional shops decline. Daventry's main streets, like those in every town, became filled with branches of banks, building societies, travel agents and charity shops. No doubt the currently fashionable wine-bars will follow. After eight centuries in the market place the market was moved to High Street, which can now be closed to traffic by gates bearing the old borough seal. The top of High Street has been narrowed and the site around the Burton Memorial has been landscaped in the modern manner. One of the objectives of the Strategy was to bring back people to live in the centre, 400 new homes being projected. In this decade new community facilities have been added in the form of the Daventry Leisure Centre and The Abbey, a new building

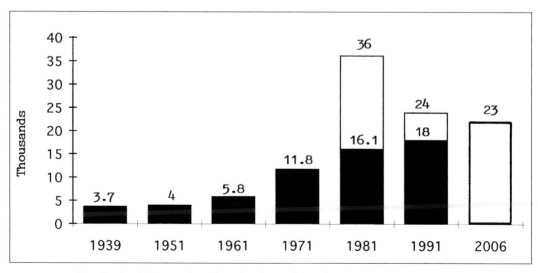

94 Graph of Daventry's projected and actual population growth, 1939 to 1991.

95 Contemporary Sheaf Street and its gazebo.

with rooms for such bodies as the Citizens' Advice Bureau and for community use. Located close to the District Council offices, these new buildings gave this part of the old town a distinctive modern look. Further out, these years saw the planning of the Daventry Sports Centre on Ashby Road in 1993, and in the same year the Council bought land on Borough Hill, opening it to public access again after two hundred years of closure.

The prudent writer should be wary of contemporary history. The immediate past takes time to fall into place and interpret. It is, however, salutary to reflect that the cliché that time marches on is true. The regeneration of Daventry has now been going forward for four decades. In common with other planned towns, Daventry has been a laboratory of social engineering. Has it proved to be a success economically, but socially and culturally a failure, as some allege? From the point of view of economics, located at the centre of the nation's communications network, Daventry has been a success, and may well continue to be so with the further integration of Europe's economy. The economic climate changes rapidly these days.

That great local mainstay, British Timken, has gone: Daventry's future success cannot be guaranteed, though the omens seem good. As to the social and cultural aspects of Daventry's transformation, it cannot be denied that there have been problems. In 1987 the newspapers carried stories of Daventry's graffiti-plastered subways, so beloved of planners, so hated by pedestrians. Daventry has also had its teenage drink problems and outbreaks of 'mindless vandalism'. In 1989 a startling rise in Daventry's crime figures led it to being awarded the dubious accolade of 'crime black spot of the county'. A flurry of police activity soon brought the statistics down. In these respects Daventry differs little from other towns, particularly other new towns. The confident expectations of the post-war planners that communities could be built from new by transplanting people from old towns, by providing better housing and by the zoning of home, work and shopping, can be criticised. But few foresaw the extent and rapidity of economic, social and cultural change which (particularly the changed job market and the rise of teenage culture) has engulfed the country since 1960. In any case,

96   Contemporary Sheaf Street, pedestrianised.

many, perhaps the majority of, people that came to Daventry found it a decent enough place to live, work and raise their families. In one important respect new Daventry was similar to almost everywhere else. Despite the avowed intentions of the planners that there should be 'a good social mix' in the new town, most of the houses that were built before 1980 were council houses, for those below the middle-class. The latter took themselves off to the surrounding villages. In this respect, too, Daventry does not differ from the norm. Since Victorian times those who could have always availed themselves of opportunities to become as detached or semi-detached as their income or inclination allowed. Village life is the modern suburban option.

Finally, in all this, can we discern any continuity with Daventry's thousand year existence? In one respect, yes. Despite the fact that its population has recently more than tripled, by national standards Daventry is still a small town. Maybe too small, if we are thinking of the opera and the ballet, pop concerts, major league sport, having a university, or whatever other facilities the well-rounded urban centre is supposed to need. Meanwhile, Daventrians will get on with their lives in a town which is small enough for people to recognise one another, and are mobile enough to take themselves off to Northampton, Coventry or Birmingham for specialised shopping, theatres and concerts.

Notes

Abbreviations used

NH *Northampton Herald*
NM *Northampton Mercury*
NPL Northamptonshire Libraries, Northampton Abington Street branch.
NRO Northamptonshire Record Office
PRO Public Record Office, London.

Two: Under Borough Hill
1. Royal Commission on Historical Monuments, *Northamptonshire, Volume 3, North West Northamptonshire*, 1981, pp. 62-72; Dennis Jackson, 'The Iron Age Hillfort at Borough Hill, Daventry: excavations in 1983', *Northamptonshire Archaeology*, Vol.25, 1993-4, pp.63-67; and 'Further Evaluation at Borough Hill', Vol.27, 1996.
2. A.E. Brown, *Early Daventry. An essay in Early Landscape Planning*, University of Leicester, Department of Adult Education in association with Daventry District Council, 1991.

Three: Daventry's Origins and Early History
1. Brown, *Early Daventry*, p.14.
2. I. Soden, 'Saxon and Medieval Settlement Remains at St John's Square, Daventry, Northamptonshire, July 1994 to February 1995', *Northamptonshire Archaeology*, 27, 1996, pp.57-99. Northamptonshire Heritage, 'Report on St John's Square', 1997.
3. Brown, *Early Daventry*, p.78.
4. *Ibid.*, pp.14, 77.
5. *Ibid.*, p.56.

Four: Priory Manors and Market: Medieval Daventry
1. Brown, *Early Daventry*, p.16.
2. M.J. Franklin, 'The Secular College as a Focus for Anglo-Norman Piety: St Augustine's, Daventry' in J. Blair (ed.), *Minsters and Parish Churches. The Local Church in Transition 950-1200*, Oxford Committee for Archaeology, 1988, pp.97-104.
3. M.J. Franklin (ed.), *The Cartulary of Daventry Priory*, Northampton, 1988, pp.xxvi, 206-7.
4. J. Baker, *The History and Antiquities of the County of Northampton*, 1822-30, Vol.1, p.327.
5. Brown, *Early Daventry*, p.16.
6. *Ibid.*, p.32.
7. *Ibid.*
8. *Ibid.*, p.27.
9. *Ibid.*, p.28.
10. *Ibid.*, pp.50-51, 56.
11. *Ibid.*, pp.81-2.
12. J.F.D. Shrewsbury, *A History of the Bubonic Plague in the British Isles*, 1970, p.104.
13. Brown, *Early Daventry*, p.36.

14. A.H. Thompson, *Visitation of Religious Houses 1420-36*, Lincolnshire Record Society, 1914, p.7, and *Visitation of Religious Houses 1436-49*, Lincolnshire Record Society, 1918, p.14; K.J. Allison, M.W. Beresford, J.G. Hurst, *The Deserted Villages of Northamptonshire*, Leicester, 1966, pp.37, 47.

Five: 'Baily Town': Tudor and Stuart Daventry

1. Public Record Office, E179/155/122.
2. J. Bridges, *The History and Antiquities of the County of Northampton*, 1791, 1, 46-7; G. Baker, *The History and Antiquities of the County of Northampton*, 1822-30, 1, 315-7.
3. NRO Topographical Notes, Daventry. Letter of 1 March 1954 from G.G.W. Bill to P.I. King on this matter.
4. R.M. Serjeantson and H.I. Longden, 'The Parish Churches and Religious Houses of Northamptonshire: Their Dedications, Altars, Images and Lights', *The Archaeological Journal*, LXX, No.279, 2nd. Ser., Vol.XX, No.3, Sept. 1913, pp.155-161.
5. H.I. Longden, *Northamptonshire and Rutland Clergy from 1500*, 1938-43, *passim*.
6. W.J. Sheils, *The Puritans in the Diocese of Peterborough 1558-1610*, Northampton, 1979, *passim*.
7. Bodleian Library, Oxford, Wase's Papers, Vol.IV, fo. 145.
8. *Calendar of State Papers Domestic*, 1601-10, 8, p.252.
9. NRO D2419, Dragge Book; Alan Everitt, *Agrarian History of England, III*, 1990, p.502.
10. Petition to Earl of Leicester, NRO YZ9118; Bridges, *Northamptonshire*, Vol.1, p.41.
11. NRO ML 755.
12. Displayed in Daventry and District Museum. For an English translation made at the time, *see* NRO Th 1497.
13. NRO Th 1669.
14. *Ibid*.
15. NRO ML106.
16. NRO 2nd Series Wills, P, p.80.
17. *Ibid*., E, 96; A.G. Matthews, *Calamy Revised*, 1934, p.7.
18. NRO Th 1673.
19. NRO D3013.
20. NRO M(TM)575/51.
21. Colin Davenport, 'Daventry's Craft Companies 1590-1675', unpublished dissertation, Leicester University, 1996.
22. NRO SG164 and 165.
23. Quoted in Alan Everitt, 'The English Urban Inn 1560 to 1760', *Perspectives in English Urban History*, ed. Everitt, 1973, p.103. For Warwick's will *see* NRO 2nd Series Wills, M 210.
24. For their part on the Corporation, *see* NRO, ML 106 and ML 755. As tenants of Christ Church, *see* Christ Church Archives, Oxford, Daventry Deeds 1649 to 1744, A1 to A17. For some details of Farmer Wills, *see* NRO Henry Isham Longden Pedigrees.
25. *Calendars of State Papers Domestic, Charles I, 1635*, p.560; *1636-7*, pp.150-1; *1638-9*, pp.43, 342; *1639*, p.472.
26. *C.S.P.D., Charles I, 1640*, pp.7, 476-7.
27. *Northamptonshire Notes and Queries*, 111, IV, 63-4 and IV, p.250.
28. Baker, *Northamptonshire*, Vol.1 p.328.

Six: 'A Town of Very Good Business': Later Stuart and Georgian Daventry

1. NRO Hesketh Baker, M55 708.
2. A.G. Mathews, *Calamy Revised*, 1934, pp.105, 523; NRO 3rd Series Wills, V, 120.
3. *Calamy Revised*, pp.29, 105, 342, and 546.
4. Daventry United Reformed Church Records. Volume of MS letters referring to Daventry Independent Chapel. In 1760 there were 45 members and in 1806 about 68. At the Religious Census of 1851 the figure for the general congregation was 260 for morning service and 320 for evening service over the past 12 months. PRO HO 195/169. *See also* volume relating to

General Charities in the Chapel records. For the schoolmaster, *see NM* 17 Nov 1820.

5. *See NM* 5 Apr 1901 for a full and scholarly account by 'JDA'.
6. *Ibid.*
7. *Ibid.*
8. For the will, *see* NRO, Butcher (Daventry), 52. For giving up the school, *see* NRO D 7810.
9. For a full analysis of the Tithing Book by the present writer, *see Northamptonshire Miscellany*, E. King ed., Northamptonshire Record Society, XXXII, Northampton, 1983, pp.62-108.
10. *Ibid.*, pp.77-8.
11. *Ibid.*, p.86.
12. NRO Diocesan Records. Faculty Register 1752, ii, fos.249, 251.
13. *Ibid.*, Faculty Register 1754, 111, fos.3-6.
14. Borough Assembly Book, 1607-1783, p.79.
15. Information from H.I. Longden, *Northants and Rutland Clergy* and The Borough Assembly Book 1783-1835, *passim*.
16. For Wadsworth, *see NM*, 19 July 1773 and 2 Jan 1796.
17. For Sanders, *see NM*, 29 Nov 1800 and *Kelly's Directory for Northamptonshire*, 1847, p.2065.
18. For the ladies academies, *see NM*, 7 Apr 1746, 29 May 1769, 11 Apr 1785 and 2 Jan 1796.
19. *Report of the Board of Education on the Endowed Charities of Northamptonshire (Elementary Education)*, 1906, Vol. 2941, p.47 and NRO DFA5, 'Account Book of the English Charity School 1722-1808'.
20. *Ibid.*
21. Borough Assembly Book 1595-1783, 29 Oct 1655, 30 Oct 1657, 4 March 1675.
22. PRO E179/157/446.
23. Borough Assembly Book, 4 April, 19 July 1681.
24. Sawbridge information largely from Baker, *Northamptonshire*, Vol.1, pp.161-2.
25. NRO 5th Series Wills. *Further Report of the Royal Commission on Charitable Bequests*, 1825.
26. *Royal Commission on Municipal Corporations*, 1835, p.1843.
27. Borough Assembly Book, 8 Jan 1676-7.
28. NRO NPL 650.
29. NRO Box X5436.
30. NRO D6343.
31. There is no complete run of accounts of the overseers of the poor. These figures are calculated from extant accounts in the Daventry Collection at NRO and in the parish records.
32. NRO Daventry Vestry Minute Book.
33. *Further Reports of the Royal Commission on Charitable Bequests*, 1825, has a useful summary of the Daventry Charities. This section is based on this source.
34. NRO Y24760 (1715 agreement). *NH* 6 Sept 1834, sale of waterworks.
35. R. Blome, *Britannia*, 1673, p.177; Celia Fiennes, *Through England on a Side Saddle*, 1888 ed.; John Morton, *The Natural History of Northamptonshire*, 1712, p.25; Daniel Defoe, *A Tour Through England and Wales*, Everyman edition, II, p.86.
36. NPL Cuttings, *NM* 3 March 1755.
37. *NM* 8 Oct 1755, 2 Oct and 26 Sept 1795.
38. *NM* 7 April and 23 June 1766.
39. NRO 3rd Series Wills, L, 247.
40. *NM* 20 May 1797, 19 Feb 1781, 23 Sept 1783, 24 Sept 1785.
41. NRO D7966.
42. NRO Parish Register 1630-1700, pp.62-3 and 123; *NM* 18 Feb 1740.
43. *NM* 1 July 1754.
44. *NM* 18 Feb 1760, 28 Dec 1767; *The Universal British Directory of Trade and Commerce*, 1791, II, 68; *NM* 7 Feb 1807 and 29 Sept 1810.
45. *NM* 6 Oct 1810. *Pigot & Cos. Directory for Northamptonshire*, 1823-4.
46. *NM* 17 Aug and 9 Oct 1752, 7 May 1753; *NM* 14 June 1760; G.H. Axler, *The Cheese*

Handbook, 1970, p.48.
47. NRO Admons, 1666.
48. NRO D2752.
49. *Ibid.*
50. For Rose, *see Bailey's British Directory*, 1784; *NM* 6 May 1786 and 17 Oct 1787; *The Universal British Directory of Trade and Commerce*, 1791.
51. *NM* 19 July 1800, 1 Apr 1840; W. Pitt, *General Survey of the Agriculture of Northamptonshire*, 1809, p.243.
52. V.A. Hatley, 'The Inhuman Taskmaster. A Story of Weedon Bec', *Northamptonshire Past & Present*, Vol III, 1960, pp.30-34.
53. V.A. Hatley (ed.), *The Northamptonshire Militia Lists 1777*, Northampton, 1973, pp.37-44.
54. *NM* 2 Mar 1752.
55. *NM* 19 May 1751.
56. *Bailey's British Directory*, 1784 and *The Universal British Directory*, 1791 *op.cit.*
57. There is a mention of horse racing in the *London Gazette* of 1696, no.3189, and annual notices on the *NM*, usually in May or June, between 1724 and 1742.
58. *NM* 4 Jan 1748, 28 Feb 1780, 18 Mar 1782.
59. *NM* 7 June 1762.
60. *NM* 2 Jan, 16 Jan and 23 Jan 1847.
61. *NM* 2 May 1787, 8 Dec 1777.
62. *NM* 9 and 30 Apr 1770.
63. *NM* 23 Feb to 20 April 1799, 12 Sept 1803, 29 Sept 1810; *NH* 24 July 1838.

Seven: Zenith of a Road Town: Daventry 1790 to 1840
1. Information of coaching from D. Mountfield, *The Coaching Age*, 1976; E. Cobbett, *An Old Coachman's Chatter*, 1891, 1974 reprint.
2. *The Universal British Directory of Trade and Commerce*, Vol.2, 1791, p.772.
3. Cobbett, *op.cit.*, *Pigot & Co.'s Directory for Northamptonshire*, 1830.
4. *Ibid.*
5. A. Bates, *Directory of Stage Coach Services, 1836*, 1969.
6. *NM* 12 July 1830.
7. *NM* 9 Feb 1799.
8. V.A. Hatley, *Shoemakers in Northamptonshire 1762-1911. A Statistical Survey*, Northampton History Series No.6, 1971.
9. *NM* 4 Jan 1907. Article on the Early History of Methodism in Daventry, by the Rev. G.B. Saul.
10. PRO HO195/169.
11. *NM* 21 Nov 1812. NPL Cuttings Collection, SPCK founded in Daventry 1815.
12. *Pigot & Co. Directory for Northamptonshire*, 1841.
13. Borough Assembly Book 1783-1835, 25 June 1829.
14. Sheaf Street Chapel, MS Minute Book of the Daventry General British School 1842-61.
15. *NH* 3 Aug 1839.
16. *NH* 13 Oct 1849.
17. *NM* 15 Dec 1792.
18. *NM* 14 Sept 1800.
19. NRO Map 1701.
20. 46 Geo III 1806.
21. NRO, Minute Book of the Daventry Street Commissioners, *passim.*
22. *Ibid.*
23. NRO, Parish Records, Minute Books of the Daventry Vestry 1750-1827 and 1827-1939, and of the Select Vestry 1819-35.
24. NPL, cutting dated 22 Mar 1783.
25. *NM* 12 Mar to 30 July 1825, *passim.* NRO YZ 8100, *Report of the Trial in which an Action was*

Brought by the Corporation of Daventry against John Dickins for refusing to purchase his freedom of the Borough, Birmingham, 1825.

26. NRO D4884. Borough Assembly Book, 23 Nov 1826.
27. *NM* 26 Mar 1831.
28. *NM* 2 July 1831.
29. *NM* 21 May, 4 and 11 June 1831.
30. *NM* 2 Jan 1836.
31. *NM* 15 and 29 Jan 1836. *The Probable Effects of the Proposed Railway from Birmingham to London Considered*, London, 1831. Written in Daventry.
32. NPL Broadsides (1-192), dated 25 Nov and 13 Dec 1830.
33. *NH* 22 Sept, 6 Oct, 10 Nov 1838. A. Cossons, 'The Turnpike Roads of Northamptonshire with the Soke of Peterborough', *Northamptonshire Past and Present*, 1950, 1, No.3, p.35.
34. *NM* 10 July 1841, 10 May 1845, 17 June 1848.
35. *NH* 12 and 19 Aug 1848.

Eight: The Long Decline: Victorian Daventry 1840 to 1914

1. The 1851 statistics are calculated from the Census Enumerators' Books. The 1886 figures are from a letter in the *Northamptonshire Guardian* 23 Oct 1886. On Stead & Simpson in 1879, *see Shoe and Leather Trades Chronicle*, 1 Aug 1879 p.25. On Rodhouse, *see Rodhouse: the History of an Old Established Boot Manufactory*, n.d. (*c*.1912), Daventry.
2. In NPL there are 12 handbills on trade disputes in Daventry between 1828 and 1854. The *Northern Star*, the Chartist newspaper, has several accounts of meetings in the early 1840s.
3. For ox-roasting at the October Mops Fair, *see NH* 26 Oct 1844. The 1868 petition is in the form of a printed handbill in NPL.
4. *Pigot's Directory*, 1823-4, *Kelly's Directory*, 1847.
5. *A Victorian Poacher: James Hawker's Journal*, ed. G. Christian, 1961, p.12.
6. *NM* 4 Nov 1865, 31 Oct 1868; *NH* 8 Nov 1879; *NM* 8 Nov 1879.
7. *NH* 8 Nov 1873.
8. *NM* 31 Oct 1890.
9. *NH* 5 & 12 Sept 1857; *NM* 23 May 1868; *NM* 12 Apr 1890 (Report of Her Majesty's Inspector of Constabulary).
10. *NH* 17 Jan 1835; *N. Chronicle* 17 Sept 1836.
11. *NM* 27 June and 11 July 1868.
12. *NH* 21 June 1871, 31 May 1873; *NM* 9 Jan 1875; *NM* 1888-90 *passim*.
13. *NM* 8 Feb 1890.
14. *Report of the Moot Hall Committee, with Appendix*, Daventry, 1879. *Northamptonshire Guardian*, 14 Mar 1885.
15. For the scandal, *see NM* 1 and 22 Dec 1888, 2 Feb 1899. For the opening of the Recreation Ground, *NM* 30 Oct 1890. And for the unveiling of the Burton Memorial, *NM* 10 Feb 1911.
16. *NM* 21 Feb 1874, *N. Guardian* 22 Sept 1883. Sheaf Street Chapel was also restored in 1880, *see N. Guardian* 18 Sept 1880.
17. NRO D2858 (town clerk's letter to Charity Commission). *NH* 2 May and 8 Aug 1857 (Corser and restoration). Mayor's letter in 1871, *Victoria History of the County of Northampton*, Vol. III, 1930, p.277. For Hutton and Logan, *see NM* 14 Apr 1888, *NH* 8 Aug 1891 and *NM* 5 Aug 1892.
18. *NH* 8 Aug 1891, *NM* 5 Aug 1892.
19. *Kelly's Directory for Northamptonshire*, 1914, p.71.
20. NRO Misc Q.S.R 308/38.
21. *NM* 15 July 1854. *NH* 23 May 1891.
22. *NH* 3 Jan 1891; *NM* 2 Dec 1892.
23. *NM* 30 Mar 1889 Formation of the Union, 1 Jan and 21 Oct 1892 (letter calling for representation on the Council).

24. *NM* 5 Oct 1889 (Volunteers at Camp), *NH* 11 Feb 1893 (2nd anniversary of the Masonic Lodge).

25. *Northampton Chronicle* 1 Apr and 21 June 1837, for start of Temperance. 'Old Daventry and the New. Then and Now 1825-1907', Cutting dated 4 Jan 1908 in NPL (? *Daventry Express*).

26. For cricket, *see NM* 17 July and 14 Aug 1858, and *NM* 7 June 1879 (Stead & Simpson match). *NM* 1 May 1875 (cycling).

27. *Kelly's Directory for Northamptonshire*, 1890 (football). For steeplechasing, *see NM* 31 Mar 1838 and adverts in March in the papers between 1872 and 1877. Horse Show adverts appeared in the paper in late September from the 1880s to the Great War.

28. For the 28th annual exhibition of the Horticultural and Floral Society, *see NM* 13 Sept 1873, *NH* 16 Aug 1856 (Gooseberry and Currant Show), *NH* 25 Feb 1893 (the Fanciers).

Nine: The Long Decline Continued: Daventry 1914 to 1945

1. *Northampton Independent* 26 May 1928 (opening of by-pass). *Kelly's Directory for Northamptonshire*, 1928, p.69 for bus services.

2. *Souvenir Programme of the opening of Daventry High Power Station Monday 27 July 1925*, BBC, 1925.

3. Derek McCormack, 'Daventry 5XX' in *Bulletin of the British Vintage Wireless Society*, Vol.16, No.4, 1991, pp.44-47. *Chronicle and Echo*, 1 Aug 1975. *BBC Daventry 1925-1992*, BBC, 1992.

4. NPL Cuttings, undated, 1926, for first Labour mayor, *Chronicle and Echo*, 6 Jan 1939, old customs.

5. Daventry Library, Dorothy Marshall, MS Social Science thesis and Advanced Geography thesis, Goldsmiths College, 1940-42.

6. *Ibid.*

Ten: Daventry Renewed, 1945 to 1999

1. This chapter is based on the large collection of newspaper cuttings in NPL.

2. Daventry Town Map. Written Analysis, 1966.

3. *Surveyor. Local Government Technology*, 12 July 1969. *Daventry Central Area Plan*, 1971.

4. Report by Peter Walker headed 'Daventry … The Expansion Town that Isn't Important Any More'. *Daventry Weekly Express*, 18 Jan 1980. Article by Mr. Bill Edwards in *Chronicle and Echo* 28 Oct 1975.

5. Daventry Town District Plan. Written Statement by P.R. Waights and K.J. O'Shaughnessy, 1980, which replaced the Approved Daventry Town Plan, 1972, of the County Development Plan.

Daventry in 1958, Ordnance Survey 1:10,000.